Well Was
Well Is
Well Be

owook

BOOKRUM
PUBLISHER

Copyright © 2025 by owook
All rights reserved.
ISBN: 979-11-6214-539-5

All rights reserved.
No part of this publication may be reproduced, distributed, or transmitted in any form or by any means—electronic, mechanical, photocopying, recording, or otherwise—without the prior written permission of the publisher, except in the case of brief quotations used in critical reviews or scholarly articles, as permitted under U.S. copyright law.
For permission requests, please contact: editor@bookrum.co.kr

All photographs and illustrations in this publication have been properly licensed by BOOKRUM directly from the original creators.
No content, including text or imagery, was generated using artificial intelligence.

First Printing, 2025

This book is a translation of the original Korean work.

Translation by Jisang Jeong
Proofreading by Bystrova Anastasiya
Book Design by Jeong Heana, Lee Jung-ah

To connect with the author and explore more of their work,
follow @owook on Instagram

BOOKRUM Publisher
36, Digital-ro 27-gil, Guro-gu
Seoul, Republic of Korea 412, 08381

CONTENTS

I
Rule the Mind

Happiness Begins in Small Things · 12

A Life of Joy · 14

Surrendering to Emotion · 16

The Heart That Lets Go · 19

Philosophies That Ground Me · 21

The Courage to Be Kind in Darkness · 25

Toward a Solid and Simple Life · 27

The Loneliness I Must Live Through · 29

Grace in Facing the Negative · 32

The Quiet Things That Hold Me Together · 35

Toward a Simple Life · 39

When Your Heart Feels Heavy · 40

A Fleeting Turn, A Flexible Thought · 43

All Be Well · 46

To You Who Cannot Sleep · 48

II
On Connection

I Seek You When I'm Sick · 52

Those Gentle in Delicate Presence · 54

Those Without Sharp Edges · 57

The Blunt-Hearted · 59

The Art of Lasting Bonds · 62

Relationships Are Defined by What We Dislike · 66

May the Meaning Stay · 68

Promises When Relationships Felt Difficult · 69

All or Nothing · 73

The Heart, The Present Once Given · 74

Sustaining Relationships · 75

What I've Learned About People, Over Time · 76

A Matter of the Heart, Not a Matter of Fault Itself · 80

If You Are to Give Your Heart · 83

I Water on Plants · 84

Don't Waste Your Time · 85

Cliff's Edge of Relationship · 87

Those Who Leave the Cut Clean · 89

Behind Glass · 92

III
The Crown Belongs to Love

Heading Toward Romance · 96

Love, Came Anyway like The Sun · 97

Indeed, saying "I Miss You" · 99

The Perfect Season for Love · 100

Letter to the One I Love · 103

The Greatness Love Brings · 107

Let's Go Together · 110

The Proof of a Kind Heart · 112

The Ideal Type · 114

This Is the Relationship I Dream with Someone I Love · 116

Someone Who Brings 'Extra' on 'Ordinary' · 122

Love is Writing or Reading · 123

When We Are in Love · 125

Besides · 127

Love Makes Time Where There Is None · 130

When Tender Tends a Tender Heart · 132

It Was All Because of Love · 136

Was Their Love Real? · 139

When Spring Comes · 140

A Matter of the Heart · 142

To You, Who Once Hurt by Love and People · 144

Perhaps It Wasn't Love · 147

Reasons for Breakups That Now Make Sense · 148

What If · 152

And So, Love Comes · 153

Mom still thinks of me · 158

To Be Called by Name, Like Her · 160

Rice Tinted with Fish · 161

The Taste of My Mother's Stew · 163

Ms. Lilac Kim · 164

IV
Stand Your Ground

Filling My Life With Things I Love · 172

What Matters Most Is Steadfast Authenticity · 176

Preserving My Whole Self · 178

I Made It · 182

Dear My Greatest Enemy · 184

A Reason to Love Myself · 187

Shape of Myself · 188

On Loving Oneself · 190

Sentence, Somewhere That Lifts You Up · 194

Can We Love Without laming? · 196

The Courage to Give Up · 202

You May Run, You May Look Away · 205

V
On Sadness and Shadows

Misfortune, Not Invited · 212

If I Could Go Back, Just Once · 214

It Was 6:40 and I Wanted to Live Like a Streetlight · 216

System Failure: Unplugging for a Moment · 220

The Inevitable in Life · 221

Sleepless Night · 224

Hearts That Open Wide · 226

The Courage to Be Kind in Darkness · 228

The Proof of a Heart · 230

What I Regret Most · 232

The Hunger of the Heart · 234

When My Shadow Stands in My Place · 236

To Be Tenderly Attached to Every Moment · 238

Days When It Seems No One Cares About Me · 239

No Matter How I Crumble, Unless I Cease to Break Down · 241

Because I, Too, Am Living as Myself For the First Time · 244

Faith, Hope, and Love · 247

Neither Sutured nor Flowing · 253

To You Who Are Someone's Light and Someone's Sea · 255

VI
We Shall Well Be

You Are Certainly Doing Well · 260

The Edge of A Coin · 261

The Worry Worm · 264

Remember When Life Feels Overwhelming · 266

Nothing Does So Just to Do So · 269

Your own Season · 271

When to Entrust the Time · 273

Life's Signposts · 276

Living Well Means · 282

Though I Can't Remember Your Voices · 284

The Green Light Towards Your Life · 286

Setting Sail · 289

I

Rule the Mind

Happiness Begins in Small Things

The small strokes of luck we meet in our everyday life, or the soft comfort we feel as we sink into bed—these are what hold our lives. Day after day, month after month, year after year, What helps me get through isn't some grand stroke of fortune or an extraordinary achievement. Sometimes, it's as simple as baking a batch of cookies, cracking an egg, and finding not one, but two yolks inside. Or the little delight of rediscovering a lost ring while cleaning, finding a forgotten lip balm tucked inside last year's coat pocket. The simple pleasure of savoring an especially delicious snack, or stumbling upon white magnolias blooming when the air still calls for scarves. The quiet warmth of securing a sunlit window seat on the bus.

This is where happiness gathers, life's satisfaction quietly accumulate—in the small and ordinary things, in the moments we might have easily passed by, in the simple, everyday details we learn to notice and hold dear.

We often believe it comes crashing in like a tidal wave, like grand strokes of fate or significant achievements. But ironically, more often, it is the expectation of such miracles that leaves us bruised. It is the tangled web of exaggerated hopes and elusive miracles.

Happiness doesn't arrive like a great tsunami, overturning everything at once—It is more like gentle waves on a beach, slowly gathering grains of white sand.

A Life of Joy

May life be joyful—not just the kind that bursts into laughter or carefree chuckles, but a deeper kind of joy. Joy isn't only the quiet hum that escapes without you noticing; it's the strength to stand firm amid life's endless adversities, to weather the restless tide of emotions at dawn, and to never surrender to despair.

It's about welcoming life's trials as stepping stones, finding ways forward, and somehow savoring the journey. Rather than crumbling under longing or sadness, it's about embracing these feelings—sometimes with even sadder songs playing in the background—and then stepping into a morning washed clean of yesterday's heavy clouds.

They say life isn't about waiting for storms to pass but about learning to dance in the rain. It is facing, again and again, the very things that threaten to undo me—slowly finding my own way through. This is the joy I hope fills my life.

For someone who once wished only for peaceful days, setting aside even happiness—how wonderful it is to feel this new promise stirring:

"May life be joyful—more, in small ways."

Surrendering to Emotion

I long to be a person who surrenders fully to emotion—who embraces every color and shade of feeling. I believe such a life is the one that shines the brightest. It means staying resolute when confronted by raw emotion. It means not letting tomorrow's anxieties make you lose the happiness right in front of you. It means daring to wail when sorrow comes, rather than dismissing your pain by insisting, "I'm fine." It means not discarding the radiant joy within your reach just because it feels too overwhelming, and not trying to rewind life in an attempt to dodge the fear that is soon to come.

In that honest acceptance of emotion, we weep and laugh, hope and despair, hurt and heal—moving through an eternal cycle. And through it all, we grow. By surrendering to emotion, by wholeheartedly receiving what we feel, we climb one stepping stone of growth after another. When joy comes, enjoy it as it is. When pain comes, accept it just as it is. Do not deny your own emotions. Do not reject either the calm or the anxiety that stands before you.

So, may you never look back on any version of yourself with regret. May you resist the urge to file down every peak and valley of feeling into a lifeless plain. Understand that emotion is not something to conquer, but something to embrace. Life, after all, rises on warm currents and sinks into valleys of cold air. And in that constant shift, we cry and laugh, through countless shifts of temperature, over and over again. There is no greater privilege than to recognize: every moment—joyful or painful—was brilliant in its own right. This very instability is life's quiet, strange delight of living. And know that And there is no truer way to live a rich, varied life than to surrender, wholly, to each emotion as it comes.

We must carry on like the wind and waves.

Like those with no place to return,

yet endlessly continuing—

Like the wind that blows and waves that crash,

Life is an endless wandering,

countless scatterings,

and waves upon waves.

Sometimes surging forward

as if the very act of living is our home,

Sometimes breaking apart

as if each shattering moment

marks our new beginning.

Living for the sake of living,

So that we might be alive as if truly living.

The Heart That Lets Go

A fisher with an impoverished heart cannot bring themselves to release a fish heavy with eggs, yet, in the bittersweet courage to let go, we come to see just how full and abundant their heart truly is.

Having lived through the entanglements of life and countless ties, they have grown a heart both tender and vast—a heart that knows the are of letting go, and the art of setting free.

So, may you not lose yourself in solitude over the moments you let someone go, the happiness you choose to get aside. Life is much like a boomerang—just as the wounds we inflict may find their way back to us as they were, to us, so too will the happiness we release in honor of a beautiful ending. Just as one wave may sweep grains of sand away, trust that another will gently return them back to shore. See this as proof of how much you have grown, and do not corner your life with thoughts steeped in shadow.

Someone, somewhere, surely envies your vast and mature heart—the heart brave enough to recognize beauty at its peak and preserve it in memory forever.

Philosophies That Ground Me

Cultivating Joy in Each Day

When life flows with ease, peaceful and fulfilling, our focus naturally turns inward to our own growth, our aspirations, and the future ahead, refining ourselves. Most anxieties and noises arise when we fixate on others instead of tending to our own path, yet true satisfaction comes from devoting ourselves entirely to our own journey. Before anything else, we must steady our hearts and cultivate joy— only then will life unveil new paths before us. Desperation rarely leads to real change. Efforts driven by impatience rarely sustain themselves.

Even in the rush of life, let's carve out small moments of play that belong only to us. Happiness isn't always found in grand gestures but in the simple act of tending to our days with warmth. There's a quiet equation in life—when we give ourselves space to breathe, impossibilities often untangled on their own.

In Not Being Loved by All, We Make Room for Love

Accepting that we cannot be loved by everyone paradoxically opens us to being loved by anyone. Giving our heart to another is also giving them the power to wound it. Thus, the courage to embrace both affection and hurt is, in itself, an expansion of the heart—one that allows us to receive kindness just as fully. True growth in love begins with acknowledging that universal acceptance is an illusion.

Near every gentle heart lies the shadow of inevitable pain, and around every lingering resentment, love hides in veil. To love is to see this truth, to embrace it, and to walk forward nonetheless.

True Excellence Begins with Honest Gaps

Those who truly understand their own flaws never lower their heads in shame.

No matter what is said about them, they stand tall—steady and unshaken.

Self-cultivation begins with honest reflection.

By nature, we are all unfinished.

Recognizing our flaws—and striving to refine them—is already the foundation of growth.

Confidence is not born from perfection, but from quiet strength to accept imperfection.

True self-worth is not built on flawlessness, but on the solid resolve to accept one's gaps and the perseverance to fill them.

Only My Thoughts Truly Belong to Me

Life taught me this:

The only lasting fulfillment is the one we find within ourselves—not the one handed to us by others. Everything we haven't discovered for ourselves may one day slip away. Yet by the same law, what we have lost may one day return. Even if we are left with nothing, as long as we hold onto the quiet confidence to begin again, the fear of loss and the urge to cling will quietly fade away. The fulfillment we find within ourselves is rarely something we can touch—It lives in thoughts, in beliefs, in silent convictions. Perhaps it is the simple assurance:"I may not be the most successful, but

I am at peace with myself—and happy.

Or the simple realization that "I do not need a crowd; just the presence of a few cherished souls."

These, and these alone, are the gifts that will never abandon us. Everything else comes and goes.

The Storm Fits The Size of Sky

I've learned that there are no trials I cannot endure. This is not arrogance— nor is it a belief belief that I am invincible. Rather, it is the quiet understanding that life's burdens seem to match the depth and breadth of the vessel that holds them. Struggles unfold at the pace of our growth

This must be what people mean when they say, **The God gives us only the burdens we can bear.** The weight of negativity floating above my days is confined to the limits of my own sight. The storms beyond my vision are not mine to weather—at least, not yet. From a distance, life appears filled with endless hardships.

Yet in truth, the only battles we must fight are the ones before us now.

The darkness that clouds my world will pass like seasonal rain. My struggles will be no heavier than the size of my world. My pain, my exhaustion—no greater than what my heart has the capacity to bear. And so, without a doubt, the day will come when I lift my eyes to find that the sky has cleared—as if the storm had never been.

The Courage to
Be Kind in Darkness

I now understand that truly kind people aren't endlessly positive or warm-hearted; rather, they are those who, despite their many dislikes, possess a profound sensitivity. They are resilient, able to endure hardships and make sacrifices, yet they seldom speak harshly or stir tension.

Their kindness is born from deep empathy, from recognizing that others might carry the same irritations they themselves endure.

Rather than allowing their heavier emotions to distort their perception, they face them head-on, determined not to be shaped by them. Their kindness doesn't flow from an overflow of affection or righteousness, but from the conscious effort to rise above the rudeness and selfishness they've encountered.

In truth, they find little joy in people, situations, work, or love, yet they persist in choosing kindness, as if in defiance of the darkness within. They resemble fairy tale heroes, enduring relentless trials for those they love, or perhaps, they are those intimately familiar with the world's shadows, striving to never become the villain. They plant seeds of hope in those around them, reminding others that even the fiercest storms will eventually pass. They are like the violet twilight that emerges only after rain—gentle, balanced, and fleetingly beautiful.

They are those who, having seen the deepest darkness, still choose the courage to shine the brightest.

Toward a Solid and Simple Life

Let life draw its meaning not from past beauty, but from anticipation of the time that lies ahead. Let the heart make itself sturdy not through support gained from others, but through honest encouragement and critique to oneself. Let emotions flow, not by the measure of passing moods, but by the depth of where the heart is pointing.

Toward this, a solid and simple life. A life where I do not cling to the past, yet use it to enrich the days ahead. A life where I do not fill my voids through others' eyes, but needs by my own hands. Where kindness or resentment alike rise not from fleeting selfishness, but from the quiet honesty that wells up from the deepest parts of my heart.

Sometimes the path seems to take us back, yet the heart knows this to be the swiftest and truest way forward. Now I understand that things easily attainable cannot sustain my life for long. Rather than chasing only what comes easily, rather than looking for a shortcut—Willing to be sincerity and integrity even when harder to hold. So we cultivate ourselves into better people—inviting kind neighbor hoods while clearing away what harms from the landscape of our lives. This, to be a solid and simple life.

What comes too easily can never bring simplicity to my days. To do what anyone can accomplish with ease stands far from true solidity.

The Loneliness
I Must Live Through

As we go on living, what often feels like being alone is not true loneliness—it is a feeling from standing in the process of coming to know oneself.

Just as a newborn would starve without a parents' hand, but a grown child finds their own food and will not perish, just as the wild, curious child who once could not read without a teacher grows into someone who opens a book alone, and finds the world between the pages—so too do we learn: that no one else can live our life for us. It is when we realize that no one will come to rescue us, that life is ultimately about becoming our own support, that this feeling of solitude takes root. When we understand that no one else can shoulder our sadness, that these emotions are ours alone to face and overcome, we see that the kindness of others is simply that—kindness, not salvation. In the end, the weight is ours to carry. That is how this sensation of loneliness arrives.

So, you are not truly alone. You have simply come to know life deeply enough to understand that your burdens are yours to bear. No one has turned away from you, nor has the world abandoned you. When solitude presses in during the quiet hours before dawn, it is not the absence of love—it is the painful acknowledgment of a truth we resist: that no one else can live our life for us.

So then—may you live it. Not because you must, but because life, in all its weight and wonder, belongs entirely to you.

What I eat becomes my body. What I love becomes my tomorrow. What I achieve becomes my name, and what I bring forth becomes my pride. What I think shapes my heart, and the words that I say leave behind my shadow.

All of it comes from me, is accepted by me, and becomes me. It becomes my surroundings, my time. There is not a single thing that does not return to me—the wounds I give, the feelings I was given, the sideways glance, the pointed finger—all will, without fail, return to me, no matter how far they wander.

Live, always remember: who I am now will surely lead me to the person I will become. Never forget that who I am now will someday shape myself.

Grace in Facing the Negative

Today, the wind is incredibly harsh. Sometimes it's cloudy. There are days when rain drizzles is mist, and others when it pours down like falling stars. Thunder and lightning make their chaotic dance across the sky—light flashing, everything rumbling with disorder. My heart follows these rhythms: sometimes plummeting vertically, sometimes sinking into endless longing, sometimes tangling my emotions into knots. Yet if asked whether these feelings will last forever, anyone would say no. They're just the emotional tides that come with each day. Though our hearts may feel helpless, swaying with the weather, would anyone truly believe it's eternal? Would they carry it as an endless worry? Surely not. This is why we can face gray skies with grace—why we need not shoulder temporary fluctuations as eternal burdens. We know it will soon be clear. I call this having grace in facing life's shadows. Just as the weather clears, so does the heart. Knowing it will pass keeps life's storm clouds from breaking us. Understanding it will end prevents the heart's wild tempests from crushing our spirit. By recognizing its temporariness, we can even cherish the rainy moments as memories. And knowing that nothing is eternal gives us the courage to move forward with optimism.

Nothing lasts forever—not your worries, not these cloudy days. So let's allow ourselves to sway, just for this moment. Soon, it will clear up. Let's look forward to the sunny days ahead.

Life's satisfaction—often depends on whether we can embrace what's temporary without clinging to it as if it were eternal. Never forget to have grace in facing the negative.

Once I believed life was a desperate race—
A frantic sprint through a long, dark tunnel,
Trying to outrun everyone else, to find the exit first.
But life isn't about escaping the darkness.
It's about growing familiar with it—
Learning to take steady, deliberate strides forward,

The Quiet Things That Hold Me Together

Those Who Know Me Beneath the Surface

The root of my struggles often lies not merely in prolonged hardship, but in the quiet longing for someone to notice how difficult things have been for me. More often than not, The burdens of life begin to ease, not because situation changes, but simply because someone understands.

This is what it means when they say life flows on, one way or another. Even when nothing is fully resolved, when balance feels out of reach, and when we are bruised from falling again and again, we endure through those who ask, *Are you okay? What's wrong? Does it hurt?*—those who tell us, *It's alright to cry*. Their presence alone keeps us just warm enough to carry on.

Through these few, precious souls who truly see me, my life holds its fragile yet steady balance.

Underlines on Hearts

Long ago, in my childhood, my father's words carried both strength and direction. In my mother's encouragement and concern, there was a quiet wisdom. The proverbs, worries, and even the occasional scoldings from those who loved and cherished me—once spoken, they slowly woven into my heart, forming the very foundation upon which my life would grow.

What I once dismissed as mere nagging has, in truth, been a remarkable guidepost for my journey. Now, as I look back on the words I was once too young and fragile to fully accept, I recognize my own shortcomings—and find myself returning to them, seeking their wisdom once more.

Where the Tears Go

They say pearls symbolize tears. A life of true strength and worth is one where we can let our tears flow beautifully. These countless moments of release, layer upon layer, transform into something as precious and multifaceted as a jewel.

A life where emotions can be freely expressed and released is like a cleansing of the soul, lightening the weight of layered sorrow. For some things cannot simply be endured—the tears we shed become the quiet support allowing us to carry on.

The Stillness in Small Things

We live in an era where happiness is often thought of as something distinct and grand. Yet, when we look closer, we realize that true happiness neither a clearly defined form nor the result of something monumental. Rather, it quietly takes shape in the small moments—an unexpectedly delicious meal by chance on a spontaneous trip, the soft comfort of a bed as we drift into sleep after workout, the rhythm of the steps as we hum along to a favorite song playing on the street, the crisp refreshment of a cold beer after a long day's work.

Happiness is layered through these ordinary, everyday moments. Life finds its balance as we dissolve clear sorrows with subtle joys. As a rule, those distinct and grand achievements transform into anxieties over what we fear to lose.

The Self I Am

Perhaps—truly, truly—this self that feels the deepest loneliness, sadness, pain, and disillusionment, that sometimes wonders, *Why am I like this? Is this the right way to live?*—is, in the end, the very pillar that holds me up most completely. What I mean is this: though my life trembles under the weight of my own anxieties, the one who has carried me through it all is none other than myself. So, don't doubt too much. I am the protagonist of my own life, the one who has led myself forward all along.

Live Well It's the Best Revenge

As we go through life getting hurt by others, we eventually reach a point where we want to put those wounds to good use, even if just a little. The ones who hurt us hope to see us crumble under anger and regret. True revenge isn't about destroying someone else—it's about lifting ourselves up. And so, we quietly promise ourselves to live so fully, if only to prove how strong we truly are.

"Don't suffer, don't fall apart. Live so well that these things become insignificant memories."

Let's seek the best kind of revenge—living the exact opposite of the broken person they expected us to be—whole, unshaken, thriving. Let's grow and evolve, even just a little, until they have no choice but to envy who we've become. This relentless pursuit of a life well-lived—so radiant it leaves them regretting ever letting us go.

Let's not waste emotions harboring thoughts of revenge. Let's focus solely on ourselves. Remember—those who hurt us want to see us crumble. Never forget that, and truly live for yourself. Let's live well.

Toward a Simple Life

One who finds joy in the small things, but is too passionate to settle for small outcomes. One who dares to feel the ache of love given and received, yet never grasps another's hand at the cost of losing oneself. One who knows how to say goodbye with poise, and walk away with a heart at peace. One who lives like a carefree wanderer, choosing their own path, yet pursues every opportunity with unwavering determination. One who, after the rain, does not simply say, "The sky is clear," but instead whispers, "Ah, it had rained"—one who remembers the clouds that once were. One who does not struggle to survive within tangled webs of connection, but holds a heart vast enough not to be bound by any web.

This is the ONE I hope to be.

When Your Heart Feels Heavy

With the Ones Who Know You

Refresh your spirit by spending time with the precious people you can truly open up to—hometown friends, family, those who shared sleepless nights and struggles by your side. While rest is something you can find on your own, there are burdens too heavy to carry alone. The presence of good people can lift even the heaviest burdens. The bonds and conversations that bring unexpected wisdom and joy are always worth seeking.

Begin Small

Instead of focusing on big changes, start by setting small, manageable goals. Overly ambitious goals may wear you down before you even get close to achieving them. Solving things one small step at a time—even if the changes seem minor—will bring a sense of accomplishment that is anything but small. These little victories, one by one, will slowly color your life with richness and variety.

Eat What You Love

While maintaining your health and body is important, don't forget the joy of indulging in the flavors you crave—sweet, salty, spicy flavors that bring comfort. Few pleasures in life carry as much weight as the happiness of eating. Remember, even a single day of indulgence can shape your overall sense of satisfaction in life.

Be on Your Side

Rather than constantly thinking, *"Everything is my fault, and others deserve the credit,"* try shifting the perspective, even just a little, to *"Maybe it's not all on me. Maybe I deserve some credit, too."* While this mindset isn't appropriate in every situation, sometimes, lifting yourself up instead of tearing yourself down can be a quiet key to relieving stress and even making the impossible possible.

Write It Down

Start keeping track of your emotions. If you've written down your feelings in the past, reconsider them. *What was I thinking back then? What resolutions did I make? What have I forgotten? What mattered most to me?* The more you document your journey, the more solidly your future takes shape.

Go Where It's Quiet

Go to the sea. If not the sea, then a quiet lake where the light dances on the water's surface. Set your phone aside, empty your mind, and let your thoughts drift. Find a place wide and quiet enough for your heart to rest. Let yourself be embraced by nature. A solo journey can offer a depth of rest unlike anything else.

Start Now

Right now. This moment, unyielding to excuses. Whether it's your surroundings or yourself—start making a change. If immediate transformation feels too overwhelming, begin by stepping outside the routine. This very moment, as you read these words, is your beginning.

A Fleeting Turn,
A Flexible Thought

There are moments that could happen to anyone, yet we often find ourselves wondering— *Why me?* When someone dear turns away after hurting us, or when a trusted person betrays us. Somehow this just happens when everything already feels fragile, the worst of life seems to arrive all at once—a wave of misfortunes crashing without pause, a string of moments that strip away what mattered. And in such moments, many find themselves searching for answers, as though naming the pain might somehow ease its weight: *So, why? How much? Why now? Why this, for me?*

But when life corners me in such a way, I remind myself to hold onto a flexible mindset—one that bends, rather than breaks, one that embraces the randomness of life. I tell myself that this is not some grand tragedy, not a story meant to shake my very existence. It is merely an accident, an instance of misfortune that could have happened to anyone. And I try to let myself hurt, but only as much as necessary. Struggle, but only to the extent that it serves me. Any suffering beyond that is simply weight I do not need to carry. Perhaps *it was just bad luck, nothing more.* And so, I steady my heart, choosing not to let this moment define my whole life.

Everyone carries their own untold stories—
I'm simply in the middle of mine. I am simply standing in the middle of mine. With this thought, I shift my world toward greater generosity, making space for the inexplicable, the unfair, and the unanswerable. Letting go of what cannot be explained—this, too, is a way of survival. For life will always be filled with misfortunes that neither reason nor understanding can undo.

At the end of a day you gave your all to—

To you, quietly wiping away your tears

May those tears not be for outdoing anyone else,

but for guiding you toward someone

closer to joy than the you of now.

I hope these tears become precious ones

Not to surpass others,

But to lead you to someone

Closer to happiness than you are now.

P.S. *For we know, without doubt,*

We shall surely live through this.

All Be Well

Today—how hard was it? How many winds shook you, and how many times did you almost fall? How often did the day push you close to breaking, just short of tears? If there were someone, just one person, who asked you those things, then maybe, just maybe, that alone would be enough.

And if today was hard—because of someone's words, because of someone's glances, because of someone's selfishness or jealousy—even so, even then, that too would be enough.

You don't have to hold back your tears for any of it. And no, you don't have to force yourself to be strong either. If you've come to recognize, deep in your heart, that what shook you held meaning enough to hurt—then once again, that too is enough.

Even in moments of happiness—when a vague fear creeps in that the joy might break—you don't need to hold onto it so tightly. You don't need to bear the weight of protecting it. To have been happy, even just in that one moment, is already more than enough.

And there will be days—when you wake and feel like crying for no clear reason. Days when you wrestle beneath the blanket of anxiety, unable to shake it off. Still, that's okay. Because anxiety often means you are carrying something precious through the dark. And if you can accept that, then once more, you are enough.

Take it all—the joy that lifted you, and the sorrow that made you pause—carry them as they are. Let them feed you. Let them steady you. Let them move you.

Whether you go on for the sake of something you long for, or because of something that once hurt you—whether it becomes your destination or your fuel—

just go on. That, too, is enough.

So let your tears come, a little more easily. You don't have to clutch your happiness so tightly for fear it might break. Let it pass through you. Let it be.

Everything will flow, just as it always has. And you—just as quietly, just as certainly—will move forward. For all the feelings that have no final stop, for all the uncountable waves that rise and fall—just as always, all will be well.

To You Who Cannot Sleep

There are nights when, for no clear reason, sleep feels further away than usual—nights when rest won't come, and the mind keeps pacing through all it carries. Maybe it's the weight of wishes that were never real, or the quiet ache of fears too deep to name. Maybe it's regret for what never came to be, or the stubborn longing for what you couldn't let go.

And what is it—which one of these thoughts, truly, that fills us so completely, keeping us wide awake through the deep hours of this night? So many minds tangled in worry, so many hearts quietly breaking. With so many of us lying awake, no wonder the night feels noisy. No wonder sleep won't come.

To those of us—to you, to me—for whom the noise outside feels strangely familiar, I want to say this:
If, after all your desperate effort, you still had to let go, then perhaps it was never truly yours to begin with. If you find yourself drawn in—as if under some quiet spell, struggling and

aching—then maybe you are striving for a beauty worthy of that ache. And if your grip holds on, even when the tendons threaten to snap, yet you still cannot let go, then maybe it is worth hurting for. But if the end of it all brings back nothing but regret—

not sorrow, not longing, but sharp-edged regret—then it must be something that would only have broken you more, the longer you stayed.

You tell it to yourself.

That after this night—this long, quiet night you and I have stayed awake through—dawn will come. That being unable to sleep means you are holding a deep hope for your life, for your future. That you are someone honest enough to feel everything your heart carries. So let me say this:

Through this sleepless dawn—all your effort, your longing, your ache, your fear, your regret—they are proof that you are living well. This is what I wanted to tell you in the quiet seam of dawn.

II

On Connection

I Seek You
When I'm Sick

There are people who come to mind whenever I'm sick. When life is peaceful and full of joy, I often forget them—but the moment I grow fragile, they return to me, gently and without fail.

Perhaps there is an unexplainable instinct of the heart, to return home. Mother, father, the roads of my hometown, the dog we once had. Childhood friends whose whereabouts I no longer know, those I love, and those I once loved. The ones who embraced me without question, the ones so familiar I could find my way to them, even when lost. The ones who stood quietly at the forefront of my life—though I rarely told them, and barely realized it myself. Perhaps they have always been there, holding me up without a word, and perhaps they will continue to do so, long into the future. Even times grow distant between us, when hearts stray around, it is tenderness—not resentment—that comes first. And they heal the ache curled deep within me, nestled where no one else could see.

Whenever the body falls ill, the heart follows to be fragile. And each time, I find myself quietly longing to return to the warmth that once held me without question. I fumble with the thought of reaching out—unsure how to ask, unsure if I should—and instead, I whisper in my heart, "How are you doing?" I now root the spring day where our paths began to part—

    letting it remain, a tender sprout within me.

Those Gentle in Delicate Presence

Some people don't feel wounds as wounds. Some heal just enough to avoid scars. But there are those whose hearts take much longer to mend. I don't see them as weak-hearted—I see them as possessing infinitely delicate hearts.

Unlike those who pull wilting flowers from vases to dry them, they are the ones who cannot bring themselves to let go, tending to fading petals with quiet devotion. They are the ones who try to make forever real, even while knowing nothing truly lasts.

They are the gentle souls who keep a finished book by their bedside, unwilling to shelve it away, opening its pages again and again out of lingering attachment. They struggle to fold away their hearts, vulnerable to endings that feel too soon.

And yet, they are the warmest of people—the ones who offer the most steadfast love to all that they cherish. Those who love with extraordinary tenderness, those uniquely gentle in staying close.

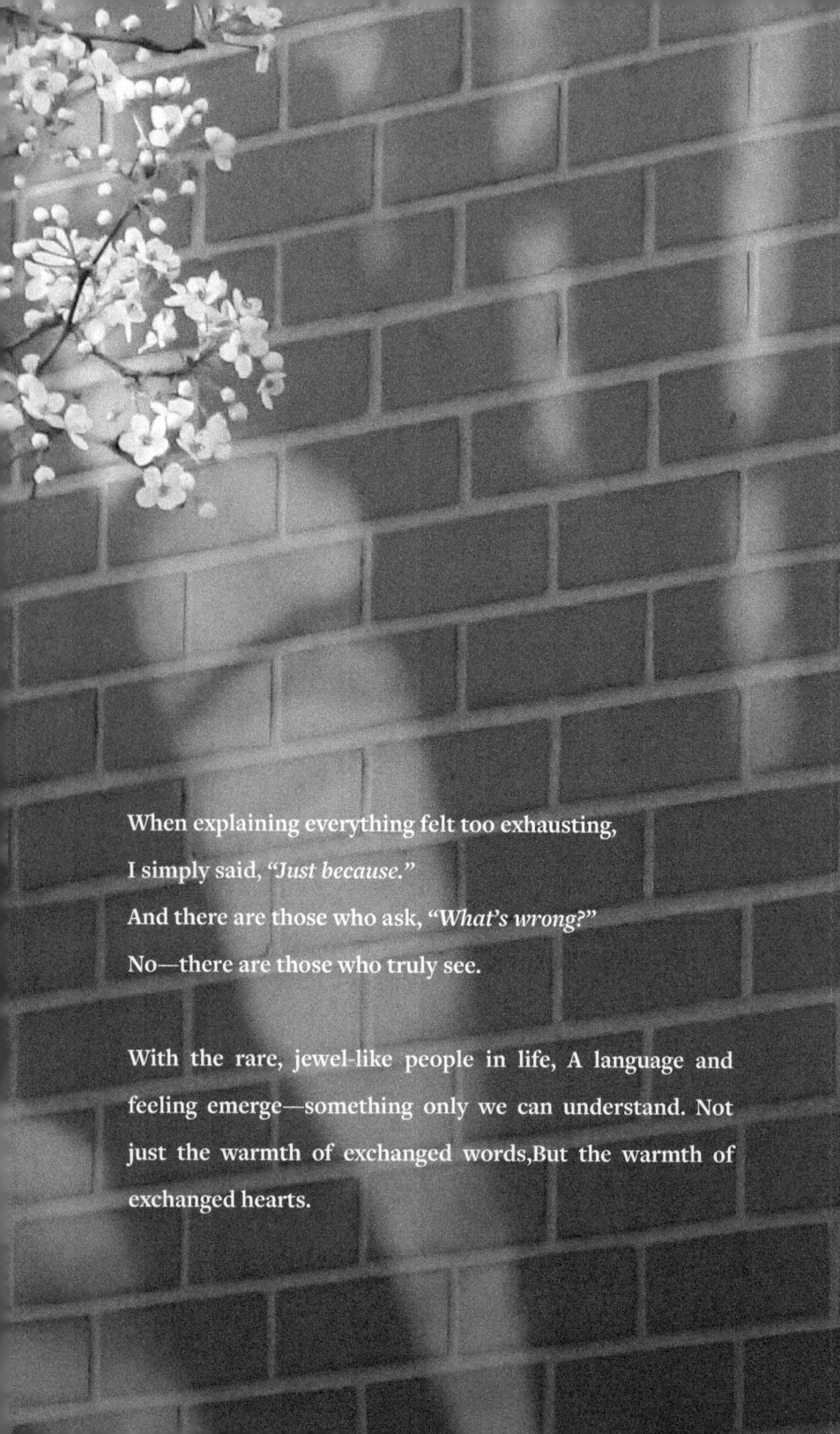

When explaining everything felt too exhausting,
I simply said, *"Just because."*
And there are those who ask, *"What's wrong?"*
No—there are those who truly see.

With the rare, jewel-like people in life, A language and feeling emerge—something only we can understand. Not just the warmth of exchanged words, But the warmth of exchanged hearts.

Those Without Sharp Edges

Not particularly sensitive to small things and with no sharp edges in their hearts, those who are often told they are "too kind" or that they should stop enduring everything are, in truth, the strongest of all.

No one is stronger than those who are often told they are too kind or should stop being so tolerant—those gentle souls who are not particularly sensitive to small things and carry no sharp edges. They have clear standards of their own, yet within those boundaries, their world remains remarkably soft and forgiving. They know how to calculate and measure like anyone else, but they choose not to—filling life's balance sheets with a different kind of equation.

These are people whose personal standards remain crystal clear, yet whose inner world is remarkably soft and unconfined. Their hearts run so deep that giving comes naturally to them, yet they hold the key to their relationships—able to walk away in an instant from those who take their kindness for granted.

Now I understand: no one wields a sharper blade than those who seem gentle and soft-spoken. In our immaturity, we may have mistaken them for easy to overlook or take advantage of. But those who have weathered life with wisdom know better.

They understand that these gentle souls have the power to break you most completely—and that their hearts should never be taken lightly.

So, to you—the one who remains consistently gentle—your loved ones surely recognize the worth of your seemingly infinite heart, your edge-free words, and your tender gestures. Though you may carry the scars of betrayal and wounds that still ache, know this: your quiet steadfastness has drawn deep and loyal supporters to your side. And in return, your gentle way of living stands as an unwavering pillar of strength for those who cherish you.

The Blunt-Hearted

There are those who remain strangely dull when it comes to their own lives. As outsiders, they listen intently to others' troubles, offering wise advice, and even present solutions—yet when it comes to themselves, they become like rusted blades, unable to make a clean cut, evading decisive action. They are accustomed to turning away from their own problems, suppressing regrets until the quiet hours of dawn, letting sighs and tears speak in place of words.

Even migratory birds remember the comfort of their nests—so why do they fail to recognize the sanctuary that would embrace them? Even a simple fish lingers near beautiful coral — so why do they keep thrusting themselves into chaotic currents? These are people who remain blunt to their own solutions, yet sharp enough to wound themselves.

But it is not out of foolishness, naive, or ignorance of the answers. Rather, they are as vast as the sky and as deep as the sea. They know all too well — but they choose to hold something even more precious. They strive to be a refuge, a place of solace for others. They cannot bear to break the bonds they cherish or taint the tenderness of memories. Their empathy runs so deep that they willingly set aside their own happiness for the sake of others. Their days often resemble the night—cloaked in shadow, quiet and unassuming.

Yet, they carry a quiet fate. One day, through this very kindness, they will find themselves bathed in the warmth of a gentle dawn.

A new white shirt, the delicate heart washing hands with soap before buttoning it up, fearing the slightest trace of dirt might stain the buttons. Like the awkward gait of walking with stiffened ankles to prevent creases from forming on the back of new shoes. Though these gestures may seem tedious or unnatural, consistently viewing someone with the same freshness as when they were new—translating that mindful gaze into action—is the wisest way to make a loved one's heart stay.

The Art of Lasting Bonds

Graceful Expression

In both everyday conversations and in moments when misunderstandings lead to hurt feelings, they never let their words cross the line. They know no relationship can rely on endless patience and tolerance alone—how something is said matters just as much as what is said. After all, a single letter can turn "united" into "untied." Just as a single word can change everything, a voice imbued with warmth and consideration can sustain bonds over the long run. Words, when tempered with care, create room for understanding and trust, encouraging both sides to keep their hearts open.

The Gift of Listening

The strongest conversations begin not with speaking, but with listening. A shared life is built on dialogue, yet when someone interrupts, dominates, or fails to truly hear, communication breaks down. Those who nurture deep relationships understand this: the art of listening is just as essential as the art of speaking. To listen fully, to offer understanding without haste—this, more than anything, becomes a quiet act of healing and support.

Flexibility with Promises

While honoring promises is essential, they understand when to offer grace. Minor lapses that cause no real harm are not held against someone with rigidity. When hurt does occur, they focus not just on the broken promise, but on the impact. The emotional energy spent policing minor breaches is too costly. By letting go of what does not truly matter, they preserve their strength for what does.

Embracing Differences

They carry a deep truth in their hearts: *This person is not me.* It is not about right or wrong, but about fundamental difference. They do not expect others to think or act as they do. In moments of disagreement, they express their thoughts and then step back—not from weakness, but out of wisdom. They know that endless arguments with someone who sees the world differently serve only to exhaust. And often, by yielding first, they create space for reflection—leading the conversation in their direction without force. A quiet yet powerful way to ease tension while earning respect.

Boundaries with Clarity

They do not avoid saying no merely to escape discomfort. Nor do they leave things vague, hoping the other person will lose interest. They understand that an inability to refuse leads only to exhaustion—for both sides. Yet, they are never unkind. When a refusal would deeply wound someone, they sometimes choose inconvenience over causing harm. To those who do not understand, they may seem distant, even cold. But in truth, their directness is a sign of deep care—they are clear because they value the relationship.

Unity Over Division

When they face conflicts arising from differing perspectives, they do not set it up as a battle between 'you' and 'me', but rather as 'us' versus the problem. Unless it's something that demands strict legal or moral judgment, they don't look for faults between themselves, but become one in seeking a solution—and relationships like this do not rust easily. When emotional conflicts arise from clashing interests, they do not point fingers, but forge a stronger bond—tempered like steel, resistant to rust. Like an icebreaker that cuts through frozen misunderstandings and stand-offs, they move forward to build a relationship—unshaken and unwavering.

Someone You Want to Keep Close

Someone who understands your wounds so deep—not to cause more pain, but to help ease your pain. Someone with whom sharing your weaknesses and innermost thoughts never leads to regret. Not just someone who comforts and encourages you when things fall apart, but someone generous enough to truly celebrate your victories.

Someone who, even in heated arguments, never makes you doubt the care underneath. Someone who, even through conflict, never pushes toward an ending—but instead, helps the bond grow stronger. Someone who faces emotions with honesty, choosing open conversation over silence. Who untangles misunderstandings before they harden, knowing that waiting for unspoken feelings to be understood only tightens the knots. Someone who respects the people around you—not seeing them as threats, but as part of the story that came before.

Someone who helps you love yourself more. Who knows when to hold you with kindness and when to ground you in reality. Someone whose warmth makes you believe in yourself and move forward with confidence.

Someone like this makes us want to keep them close—and inspires us to become that kind of person ourselves.

Relationships Are Defined by What We Dislike

Relationships are shaped more profoundly defined by our dislikes than our likes. Consider two individuals with only a mild connection—sharing similar interests might only result in them being casual acquaintances or, worse, competitors.

However, when they discover a mutual dislike, they can unexpectedly become allies, united by this shared sentiment. We might tolerate someone disliking what we love, but it's far harder to accept when they cherish what we despise. Even with those we once held in high regard, this realization can create an unbridgeable rift.

Human relationships are often more influenced more by rejection than by affection. This is why we sometimes find ourselves resenting someone for no clear reason, or feeling inexplicably disliked. It's why, no matter how much kindness we offer, some will still dislike us—and why, even without trying, others will stand by us. We have all, at some point, both suffered from and contributed to this cycle at one time or another.

To navigate the complexities of human relationships, we must proceed with care—guided not by deceit or ill intent, but by thoughtful awareness. The most important thing is to safeguard the ones we care about, avoiding needless strife

If you love someone, understanding what they dislike, rather than just what they love, may better preserve the warmth of your bond. Sharing what we love may spark passion, but it is the absence of what we hate that keeps the embers glowing.

To maintain a lasting friendship, it's wise to prioritize knowing—and never speaking of—the people your friend dislikes rather than those they admire. Over time, our preferences will shift, but what deserves our closest attention is always what someone cannot stand.

In any setting—be it school, work, or a group dynamic—maintaining favorable relationships often hinges on understanding the unspoken dislikes that define the social environment.

We all find ourselves woven into the complexities of human relationships. Amid the inevitable challenges they present, perhaps the wisest approach is not to seek gain, but to steer clear of unnecessary loss.

Being mindful of one thing someone dislikes may carry more significance than a hundred acts of kindness. A shared aversion can bring two people closer than a hundred mutual joys. Standing together against a common adversary can forge a deeper connection than standing beside someone a hundred times.

May the Meaning Stay

Do not offer advice
If your heart does not ache as you speak.
Do not boast
If you are unwilling to pay the price of pride.
Love only if when you can love yourself first.
Seek forgiveness,
With the solemn knowing that it may not be yours to receive.
Express anger,
Only after measuring the weight of severed ties.
Make requests,
With the courage to accept refusal.
Say no,
Only when you can bear the sorrow of disappointing another.

May we never lose our sense of righteousness in the exchange of words, in the offering of hearts, in all the ways we try to live well. Let us not forget—Nothing holds true value unless its cause and conditions are met.
For life is filled with things we must not attempt, if we cannot do them with care.

Promises When Relationships Felt Difficult

Know When to Walk Away

There are moments when you just know—you and this person will never share the same path again. Perhaps your lives have grown too different for meaningful conversation, or you have seen something in them that you cannot accept. When that certainty strikes, I choose silence over confrontation. Even if there is a minor cost to bear, I pretend not to notice and let it go. Engaging in unnecessary disputes, weighing right and wrong, calculating every loss and gain—these are weights I refuse to carry.

That energy is better spent elsewhere, on something that nourishes my life instead. This is how I preserve my peace amid relationships that must continue out of necessity.

Those Who Cannot Say No Become Life's Greatest Burden

The people I most wish to avoid—not because they have wronged me, but because they drain my energy—are those who cannot give a firm "no."

Some people twist their words, exaggerate their struggles, or fabricate excuses to avoid direct refusal. In doing so, they wound others unnecessarily, creating hurt and resentment that simple honesty could have prevented. Why collect unnecessary resentment? Excuses born from guilt serve no one. So when I must decline a request or foresee an unmet promise, I state my decision plainly, without hesitation. It is the kindest way—for myself and for them.

Harmony Comes from Single Notes

In any well-functioning group, the unspoken rule that keeps everything intact is that each person fulfills their role. Some exist in careful symbiosis, like crocodiles and plovers. Others move forward together, finding strength in their shared burdens, like partners in a three-legged race. But still, the world runs best when each person focuses on their own responsibilities. Kindness is admirable, but spreading oneself too thin, meddling where it is not needed—these things often do more harm than good. Simply doing one's own part is often the surest path to stable, enduring relationships.

Not Every Moment Needs a Laugh

I have learned to be mindful of laughter that slips out at the wrong time. The nervous chuckle at the end of a sentence. The unthinking grin in response to something trivial. Laughter, when misplaced, can turn a simple moment into an awkward one, or make light of something that deserves weight. Most of the time, laughter is voluntary, even if it feels like a habit.

If it emerges too often, if it surfaces unconsciously in the wrong moments, it is a habit worth correcting. Especially in conversations outside the intimacy of family and old friends, where understanding runs deep, unnecessary laughter can be enough diminish credibility eroding the foundation of a professional or distant relationship.

If It Feels Off, It Probably Is

When you sense that it's better to untangle yourself from someone, when your gut tells you to walk away—ironically, it is often right. Not every instinct is flawless. Not every suspicion is infallible. And yet—my instincts are mine. I once felt someone subtly mocking me, the sting of veiled condescension in their words. Yet those around me defended them—

> "That's just how they are. They don't mean anything by it."

But even if their defense is objectively valid, if it feels subjectively wrong to me—then it is wrong. Their tone, their choice of words, the way they move within my world—if these things do not align with my sense of respect, then I have no reason to dismiss my own discomfort. Relationships exist within the realm of the subjective. What feels tolerable to one person may be unbearable to another. Others may excuse, explain, or justify—but my instincts are my own, and I have learned to trust them.

People Aren't Possessions

How wonderful it would be to be surrounded only by those who support us.

But life is not so simple. For every ally we gain, it seems we acquire adversaries in equal measure. I know how precious the few I hold dear are.

They are worth more than jewels, worth more than anything I could ever hope to replace. But when I take a step back, when I look at relationships from a broader lens, I remind myself— People are not possessions. An asset is something we cling to, something we try to keep, something we expect to remain in our grasp. But a resource is fluid, something that moves, that circulates, that was never truly ours to own. Attachment, expectation, obsession— these things leave only disappointment and scars. When relationships become too heavy, too difficult to hold, I remind myself:

People are not meant to be kept. no one was ever mine to lose.

All or Nothing

My mother always said that nothing is more graceless than giving, only to later make it known—turning generosity into a debt. That isn't virtue, she said. That's a kind of vice. It is better not to give at all than to give in such a way.

"If you lend, do it as if you are giving it away. If you give, do it as if you'll never bring it up again. Never put yourself in a position to be resented, whether in giving or receiving.

If you can't do that, neither give nor take. If you choose to yield, yield completely. If you choose to offer, offer fully. Even if you long to receive, never take what you cannot repay. And if you have the heart to give, do not let your own lack make you stingy."

Whether in giving or receiving, only doing it right keeps your heart pure.

The Heart,
The Present Once Given

The human heart is like a precious gift—once lost, it can never return to its original state. Just as a lost gift, even when replaced with an identical one, it loses its original meaning, leaving us unsatisfied despite its perfect resemblance. Trying to reclaim a lost heart is a futile effort. For both the giver and the receiver, it can never again be that precious exchange of hearts from that moment.

So, do not treat the heart you've been given carelessly, blinded by the comfort of familiarity. Nor should we struggle to hold on to hearts that were never meant to be gifts. Remember, once a heart is lost, it cannot be restored to its former self. It is because we cannot turn back time that each moment becomes so precious and beautiful. Keep this truth close, always cherish what you hold, and if a heart has already departed, do not linger in regret trying to call it back.

Sustaining Relationships

Having shared affection for a long time should never become an obligation to endure disappointment and pain. The mere duration of a relationship cannot justify tolerating indifference or selfishness. I believe that the most fragile relationships are those that attempt to excuse words and actions simply by the weight of time.

In human bonds, nothing is as perilous as the illusion that longevity equates to strength. For both the giver and the receiver, time distorts perception, bending the heart's compass until truth becomes impossible to discern.

Remember this:
What sustains a relationship is not the time spent together, but the sincerity that endures. The true measure of a relationship is not in how long we have walked side by side, but in how clearly we can still envision a shared future ahead.

What I've Learned About People, Over Time

Without Reason, With Grace

"What do you know about me?"

—This question shaped the way I saw relationships throughout my youth. What do you know about me to like me? To judge me? To comfort me? I carried a quiet aversion, believing that words from those who barely knew me were nothing but hollow pleasantries. So I tried not to listen, dismissing their kindness as shallow. But as time passed, I began to see—one doesn't always need deep understanding to feel for someone. Through countless experiences, my once-rigid walls softened. Sometimes, emotions need neither reason nor justification.

We may like someone without truly knowing them, or dislike them for the same reason. We may want to embrace someone precisely because we don't know everything about them—or turn away for that very reason. I've learned to approach people with generosity, with grace that does not demand explanation. I no longer wish to lose meaningful connections to needless suspicion, nor do I wish to hold on to others to the point of losing myself. Sometimes, it is enough to quiet my doubts and simply see people as they are.

Infinite Tenderness In Finite Time

There was a time when I resisted the truth that nothing lasts forever. From the small things—the texture of a favorite sweater, gifts given on cherished days, handwritten letters, flowers—to the significant ones—friends from childhood, parents, grandparents, beloved mentors, loyal pets who waited for me at the door.

I wanted to keep them all by my side, eternally. But time moved forward, indifferent to my longing. The idea of parting from those I could never love enough filled me with fear, with sorrow. But now, I accept—at least, a little.

If there were no end, would love ever to feel this deep?

These things we wish to hold forever—we treasure them more because they cannot stay. Because our time together is finite, we love infinitely.

Because we cannot keep them forever,
we love as if we could.

Closing My Ears, Shielding My Eyes

My life often presents moments of anger—most of them stemming from human relationships. But I have found an odd relief in not knowing everything. Ignorance, at times, has been a quiet guardian, keeping my life at a manageable balance. If someone insists on bringing me distressing news, I must learn to refuse it. If their words hold no truth, I must tell them plainly—

"You don't need to burden me with things I cannot change."

Above all, I must distance myself from those who, under the guise of care, do nothing but bring me turmoil. What troubles us most is often not what happens—but the people who amplify it, who insist on handing us pain we never asked to carry. The older I grow, the more I realize—ignorance truly is bliss. And so, in the chaos of human entanglements, there are times when the wisest thing to do is to shield my eye and turn a blind.

Finding True Friends In Times of Joy

It is easy to recognize the people who stood by us in hardship. But equally precious—perhaps even more so—are the ones who celebrate with us in joy.

Life's seasons of bloom are more vibrant than its seasons of uncertainty. And in those moments, the ones who remain by our side shine even brighter in our memory. While every form of companionship holds its weight, I have come to see— it takes a rare kind of heart to offer true congratulations without envy, to celebrate another's success without reservation. Such sincerity, given freely, is among the purest forms of kindness.

To Grow Good, To Know Good

Your energy attracts your tribe—or so they say. I once held this belief close to my heart, convinced that becoming a better person would naturally bring only good people into my life. But now, I understand that this was merely a comforting illusion. No matter how much we grow into our best selves, those who wish to harm us are bound to appear in our lives. Like insects drawn to ripe fruit, some will approach with ill intent—seeking to diminish our joy or take what is not theirs. Yet, there is profound wisdom in continuing to cultivate goodness within us. The journey of self-improvement teaches us to discern those who resonate with our values from those who do not. As we grow, we develop the insight to strike a balance between embracing meaningful connections while setting the boundaries we need. The commitment to be changed—though it may not fulfill the promise that "your vibe attracts your tribe"—remains a necessary journey we must undertake. For while it cannot guarantee that only good people will enter our lives, it shapes us into someone with the wisdom to recognize true relationships and the strength to preserve them.

A Matter of the Heart,
Not a Matter of Fault Itself

Sometimes, we convince ourselves that a relationship ended because of a single moment—because we "said that" or "did this" —leaving us fixated on the past, wishing we could undo it.

But remember: nothing erodes self-worth or casts a shadow over future relationships more than blaming ourselves for ordinary words or actions at the end of a relationship This kind of self-blame only makes us more guarded around others, causing us to lose sight of our own perspective in relationships.

When it comes to relationships, it's wise not to overestimate the weight of our own words and actions. Even if they point to that reason, more often than not, it's just an excuse. To those who dislike you, everything you say will be wrong; to those who love you, even your flaws will seem endearing. Relationships are shaped by the movement of the heart, not by mere words or actions.

Never forget: the heart is always the truest reason. And even if when you reflect on yourself, do it in a way that helps you move forward—one that allows you to remain whole through every relationship.

Life is like a train running along a long track—some people get off, some get on, and some ride all the way to the final station. It's futile to rush or force connections. Fate is beyond our control. So don't try too hard. Accept gracefully and let them flow. When sadness comes, run forward with strength. To the next station.

If You Are to Give Your Heart

If you are to give your heart, do not lend it. Know that a heart given earns no interest, know it may never return—like something cast away. Even when it makes you sad, even when you don't receive as much as you've given, accept that this is their best offering of heart. If you are to give, you must be able to hand it over with its holes intact, without begging them to overflow and fill the empty spaces where your heart once was. Acknowledge that all of this was not their selfishness, but your choice. A heart is not something to be lent—it must be given. Let go of that burning desire to reclaim the heart you've given, and be ready to offer it freely toward someone else's heart. If they are truly worth giving your heart to.

1 Water on Plants

Relationships are like plants— they flourish with care and wither in neglect. A bond between two people does not grow or wither on their own. Even resentment is a form of misplaced attention, while withholding attention is simply offering indifference. In this way, relationships are always an exchange— of presence or absence, care or neglect. If a relationship refuses to bloom despite our devoted efforts, its roots must have already rotted. But if it grows abundantly from even the smallest kindness, recognizing and returning our care many times over— then that is someone we must not let slip away. So do not torment yourself over truths your heart already knows. a bit more poetic Do not pour your heart into a bond whose roots have long since decayed. Do not make excuses or seek blame when the care you offered found no place to take root. Do not cling desperately to endings already foretold, nor stifle something that is flourishing by refusing to let it grow. Few things are as stark, as undeniable, as the vines that stretch between us. And just like plants, relationships can only truly thrive. when given exactly what they need— at the right time, in the right balance, with just the right touch.

Don't Waste Your Time

Nothing is more futile than seeking approval from those who have already chosen to dislike you. Do not waste your energy on those who resent your laughter and scorn your tears. Do not trouble yourself with people who call your efforts desperate, only to mock you for giving up. things drain time and emotion more. Do not cling to relationships that require you to grind yourself down just to be enough.

Do not hold on to relationships that demand you carve away yourself just to be accepted. When understanding remains impossible despite your best efforts, that is not mere indifference—it is disdain, a distortion in how we see one another. Just as the heart cannot be bought, love cannot be forced. And even if freely given, if its worth is never recognized, then what exists between you was never strong enough to last.

Even if I have 99 flaws, there are those who will recognize the one strength in me. And even if I have 99 strengths, there are those who will search for the one flaw to tear me down. There is no need to grind yourself away just to shine like a jewel for those who refuse to see your worth. It is enough to live among those who truly recognize you.

Live as a jewel to those who recognize your worth. Not a stone to those who never cared to.

Cliff's Edge of Relationship

I have often found myself on the side that holds on—gripping tightly when a relationship teeters on the edge. I once chastised myself for this, mistaking it for foolishness, even weirdness. But now I see—This is not folly. This is the strength of an honest heart.

Some cannot let go, even as their hearts break, even as others walk away. But I no longer see them as the abandoned or the left behind. They are the ones who have endured love at its most relentless. And now I know—those who once held on with every fiber of their being, who gave all they had before finally turning away, are the ones who carry fewer regrets when time has passed.

This, I have come to believe, is the path toward a more whole and resilient heart. What once felt like weakness in those relationships was, in truth, the preparation for something deeper, something greater. The ache of holding on was never in vain—it was making space for deeper bonds and a fuller life ahead.

And so, with newfound understanding, I embrace the heart I once was—the one that held on, not out of foolishness, but out of the courage to love fully.

Those Who Leave the Cut Clean

There are those who leave nothing behind not even a trace of attachment. Or, perhaps they are simply the kind who can only say goodbye once their heart has fully let go. They have never uttered farewell without weight, so when the time comes, it bears heavier than most. From afar, their silence after an ending may seem like a clean severance—almost too sharp to be kind.

But now I understand: With hearts like deep-rooted trees, they branch only after giving everything they have, pouring themselves into the bond with absolute sincerity.

And with time, they become the kind who can miss those they've let go, who can speak simple gratitude without weight. They leave behind seams so smooth and clean, you might long to piece them back together, captivated by the way they understand how things can take root again.

They are the ones who once believed a story had reached its beautiful ending—only to tear the final page with their own hands. And even if they grieve what was lost, they still know when it must stay lost.

Goodbye, They do not tremble after goodbye, but stand still—like a stem that's weathered the wind. Not with the stillness before a storm, but with the quiet peace that follows in its wake. Even when the remnants of a past relationship cut deep into their heart, they endure the pain in silence, knowing how to swallow it whole. These are the ones who carry a calloused courage, the kind forged on solid ground to face the end, and still stand strong.

As I drift away from the friend I was once closest to,

their closest friend quietly shifts.

As I begin to see more of someone I once barely knew,

the shape of my closest friendship changes too.

The one I loved most turns into a stranger in an instant.

And the one who was once a stranger,

suddenly share breath.

Perhaps this is the simple truth—

A truth that, once accepted, makes everything easier.

No friendship is eternal.

No love is eternal.

No person lasts forever.

Behind Glass

Even when we choose to hide behind a window, there are moments when we feel as though the world has left us completely alone. There are times when the unchanging flow of relationships, the endless cycle of love, and the stagnation of life feel suffocating and frightening, making you want to close your own window, retreat inward, and shield your heart from the world. I stand with those who need to hide. I see the isolation framed around you. But don't stay there for too long. There is someone waiting outside, and someone who stands there, hoping for the day—you will open it wide. Someone who reaches out, like salvation itself, pulling you from the depths of sorrow. Someone who refuses to give up on you. So don't stay hidden for too long. Don't stay too long in the belief that the world has turned its back on you. Even when the window is shut tight, never forget— it's still made of glass.

III

The Crown Belongs to Love

Heading Toward Romance

In a world where romance feels all but gone, sharing both sides of a pair of earbuds, listening to one song, split between our ears. Saying "I miss you" between small stories heard through the phone, then falling silent for a long while, our hearts quietly trembling. Fighting off sleep, only to drift off with the phone still in hand. Walking down festival-lit streets, our hands clasped, a small gift each tucked in the other hand. Underlining a line in a poetry book we love, and giving it as a gift. Circling the same place again and again, walking in step, reluctant to part. Printing a photo we just took, writing a short note on the back, and sharing it between us. Aren't all these the last fragile traces of romance left in the world of you and me?

Since our meetings aren't for show, they needn't be grand. Since there's nothing to prove, there's no need to explain. Steadily moving toward a romance whose temperature only we know. Steadily developing language and tenderness only we understand. Though eternal love may not exist, though the world largely lacks romance, still wanting to believe in eternity and romance like fairy tale protagonists. That is love.

Love, Came Anyway like The Sun

Once, I wandered dark night streets searching for love. Through the long hours before dawn, I would fill my room with light—one that would not be easily chased away.

Yet somehow, morning always arrived on its own, and my room would fill with sunlight as if the night had never been. Even the curtains I had drawn so carefully against brightness proved useless before the sun. Light seeped through the fabric, and when I stirred, creating small winds, the dancing rays would wake me with their brilliant ripples.

This was the love I had longed for so deeply. I had searched for it, trembled with loneliness through long dawns yearning for it. But true love, like morning arriving at its appointed time, comes when it's meant to. Just as night passes through dawn into morning. It comes to us naturally. And it was an unstoppable force. Something that would lift me, ready or not—I could not escape the love that shone upon me.

I lifted my drowsy body, gazing at the light that woke me. I squint against its brightness, raising a hand to shield my eyes. Yet my fingers are too small to block its radiance.

Love does not come simply because we desire it. Yet it arrives naturally. Something that can't be sought. Can't be replaced. Can't be controlled. Something that wakes us. Raises us up. Can't be hidden. Guides us. No matter how hard we try to block it, it keeps seeping through to illuminate us.

Someday, love comes. I shield my eyes from its overwhelming brightness. Yet the warmth slipping through my fingers tells me—I will never be able to stop it.

Indeed, saying "I Miss You"

To say "I miss you" is, in truth, to say "I love you."

Or perhaps it's a way of saying "I care for you deeply" —a quiet plea to make time, a drowsy invitation to lie together. It's an offering, a piece of one's heart given willingly. It's a gesture of solidarity, an unspoken agreement to share meals and live with fullness. It's encouragement to shake off the dust that life settles on us and witness beautiful things together.

It's an offering of the heart to grow closer, a joining of hands to simply be together. It's an invitation to find a spark of romance in a weary life, a gentle temptation to escape the monotony of routine and embark on a journey. It's an embrace asking to experience something once more, a forgiveness of one another, a quiet request to meet each other's gaze. It's a confession—a lament that solitude has become frightening.

Indeed, to say "I miss you."

The Perfect Season for Love

They say people fall in love most easily in the season they were born. It's not backed by statistics, but just something someone born in a season like mine, once told me. Perhaps, like all creatures with homing instincts, humans too have an instinct for love.

Even if it isn't true, it's a story I want to believe. That those born from love would somehow know when it is their time to love, becoming their gentlest, most affectionate selves when the season calls for it.

I was born in April, they in March, and we fell in love in May. Though the city is crowded with towering buildings, though we live lives so rushed that even a greeting to a neighbor feels like a luxury, I still believe that the seeds of romance persist. That somehow, even in the cracks of hardened asphalt, flowers will push through and bloom. That we, too, found a way to clear a small forest of love within the seasons we were given. And that we discovered a beautiful reason to explain it all.

We were born in seasons neither too hot nor too cold. And in a season just like this, we fell in love.

I always knew it wasn't true that idea about people loving in the season they were born. But still, I came to believe it, as if I had stumbled upon some hidden truth. After all, we were born in such seasons, and we fell in love in such a season, the perfect excuse. And at some point, without even realizing it, we both found ourselves believing in that romantic little lie.

"Wake up early... to love."

"Wake up early to love?"

It was January, with the New Year celebrations still in the air. We were at the exhibition you had wanted to see, and in the guestbook, someone had written:

[*Wakeupearly...tolove.*]

You looked at me, curious.

"What does that even mean?"

"It's a goal," I said. "Waking up early just to 'get by' sounds too dry. So instead—to love. To wake up and direct your heart toward something."

You grinned, amusement dancing in her eyes.

"That's so like a writer,"

you said, her gaze warm and unwavering.

Ah. Wake up early... to love.

Letter to the One I Love

* Our story won't always be filled with nothing but happiness. Many obstacles will stand before us, and countless trials may try to pull us apart. But I believe that once we get through them, even these hardships will become memories we hold dear—moments we can share warmly when we look back. We're no longer alone; together, we can face anything and transform every trial into something meaningful. So even when things get tough or we feel tempted to give up—let's hold on, side by side. May every path we walk and every hardship we overcome leave us with nothing we'd want to throw away, but only treasures we can keep close to our hearts—not a single step, not a single moment, without meaning.

* When you feel anxious even for a moment, I carry that anxiety with me for hours. If you're upset for hours, I find myself weighed down by it for days. We lean on each other so much that we become each other's greatest hope and biggest worry, the gentlest solace and the deepest sorrow. Sometimes, we are like a calm lake for one another; other times, we are like rough waves crashing toward each other. We shake each other's hearts, shape each other's days. But when one of us is unsteady, the other becomes the firmest hand to keep us from falling. May we remember this always—that we can be each other's deepest wound and yet also each other's strongest comfort. May we hold each other, not just gently, but with the courage to embrace even the weight of our scars.

* We now have so many expectations of each other. After all, how could it ever be easy for two lives to become one? In the process of adjusting, of bridging our differences, there will be words exchanged that neither of us wants to hear. When that happens, I hope we do not close our ears and dismiss them as nagging. I hope we listen, understanding that it is a necessary part of this journey. It won't always be easy to accept every word, but let's trust that they are never spoken in vain. These words are not walls, but bridges— built to strengthen us. May we always listen—not just with

our ears, but with hearts that refuse to turn away.

* We've talked so often about traveling together, yet we always ended up putting it off for "later" because life got in the way. But this time, let's leave behind our busy realities for a moment and just go—right now. I want to whisk you away somewhere. The more tangled our minds get and the less time we have, the more we should simply pack up and leave. Without elaborate plans, without second-guessing. Because what matters most isn't where we go or what we do, but who we do it with. When the world grows loud and we're tired of the noise, let's find a quiet place—any place—where we can be still, hold each other, and remember what peace feels like.

Come away with me—just you and me, right now

* No matter what happened in the past or what rumors might linger, I believe in you. Even if you stumble in uncertainty and doubt, I still believe. I trust who you are, I trust your choices, and I trust in the future we'll create together. In a world where believing in ourselves is already difficult, maybe that's the most precious reason I stand by your side. And I believe you trust me as much as I trust you. In this unpredictable world, having someone to rely on and

believe in—no matter what—feels like a miracle.

I trust you. And together, we stand—unshaken, unwavering.

* You are the someone I miss the moment I turn away, even when resentment lingers in the air between us. We may clash out of frustration or bitterness, but it's never because we truly hate each other. Love isn't always sweetness and gentle words; it can also emerge through heated disagreements and moments of tension. May we recognize these intense collisions and differences as another expression of tenderness—another way of saying, "I care." May our love embrace every flavor—sweet, bitter, and all that lies in between—so that we can grow together without skipping a single taste.

The Greatness Love Brings

I believe that loving someone brings us joy in both giving and receiving. Yet at the same time, I don't deny that this may only be a small piece of the greatness that love as an emotion can achieve.

The most valuable experience is learning to love myself—this self that my partner loves—and watching them learn to love themselves as well. When we fell in love, we each came to appreciate ourselves more deeply, each as an individual. Through love, we discovered the kind of love that makes you appreciate yourself more, that inspires you to become a better person.

It's like two once-isolated forests slowly intertwining, each so enamored with its own ecology that they end up sharing new ways of evolving with one another. I see this as one of love's rarest and most delicate miracles, second only to "sacrifice"— you might call it a form of "mature independence." It's not just about being safe within the fence called "us," but also about each person learning how to love themselves on their own.

Simply giving and receiving does not make a relationship eternal. True eternity needs a miracle worthy of the name—experiences so profound that they last forever. I believe love's true greatness lies in the miracle that makes such moments possible.

"I loved you so deeply that, in the end I learned hofw to love myself."

Harsh words spoken to someone you love dare not actually piercing the other but handing over a knife handle, something that will stab me sharpening a blade toward myself.

I wonder: did that person truly love me?

Let's Go Together

Let's go together. These words hold such weight far greater than they seem. More than listing what I love about you, more than making promises of love. I want to say them in a way that makes logic irrelevant—beyond what you can give me or what I can give you, beyond even what we may learn from each other along the way.

Let's go together.

Even if a desert stretches before us or the lake ahead is lined with fragile ice. Even when winter fades and spring follows, let's still go together. Even as petals drift, snow blankets the earth, rain washes the roads, and leaves scatter—still, let's go together.

And one day, when we've circled the world enough times for our legs to grow weary, there's one thing I hope to hear from you. That you didn't walk beside me all this way because you believed in the words *"let's go together,"* but because you believed in *me*. Then I will have just one answer for you: I walked with you not to fulfill a promise, but to hold onto you.

Now, shall we sit in the twilight, watching each other fade like the setting sun, calling it beautiful, and walking the final lap together? Or shall we wander this place again, just a little slower this time? No—the world turns anyway. So shall we lie here, hand in hand, and let the stars weave us into the sky?

The Proof of a Kind Heart

Someone who never takes even the smallest gesture of care for granted, and never overlooks my consideration. Someone whose waiting may be brief, yet leaves echoes that linger long in the heart. Someone whose heart is vast enough to offer comfort not just through sincere words, but through the solace of genuine listening. Someone who, while focused on present joy, never forgets the hardships we've shared in the past. Someone who, even when distance grows between us, has the courage to take the first step to close that gap. Someone who needs me not out of necessity, but because their heart holds genuine affection for who I am. Someone in whose presence we both reveal our true selves, not the masks we wear—creating a relationship so comfortable and unguarded that we can simply be. A connection where this ease stems not from carelessness or familiarity, but is treasured in memory as something precious. Someone whose positive nature influences me so deeply that I find myself wanting to become a better person.

If you find such a person, it's a testament that they are truly special—someone you must not let slip away.

The Ideal Type

I'm not someone who defines an ideal type in clear terms of form or condition, what might be called an "ideal type", So when asked what mine is, I usually just say, "someone I'm drawn to." But I believe attraction to a stranger doesn't come from something as categorical as an "ideal type." It's more like the invisible pull between metals and a magnet—a force you can't see with the eye, but feel all the same. So maybe it's not an ideal type, but more like an ideal state.

As life goes on, I've come to realize that in love, it's not so much the form of a person I long for, but the ecology of the relationship. We chase after clear silhouettes—the well-defined outlines of a "type." when we're young. But now we become attuned to the things we can't quite see as life goes by: what kind of environment we could share, what kind of dynamic we could build. The mind begins to move in quieter ways, in accordance with criteria that no one else may know, and the switch that once flipped clearly becomes blurred.

In that sense, the relational ecology I desire is one where both people's inner worlds are respected. Someone who can sit beside me in the same room and enjoy their own hobbies while I enjoy mine. If I had to name an ideal type, I'd say this: someone who treasures their own preferences just as much as they would a person they love. Someone who knows how to love themselves—and in that self-love, can offer a kind of love that doesn't encroach, but honors. I've always been a bit of a wild creature by nature. When someone trespasses my territory and disrupts what I love, I bare my teeth and growl. Humans, after all, are animals too. And like any creature, we long for the sanctity of our own space.

I'm drawn to someone who can quietly enjoy what delights them—even in shared spaces. Someone who can also, now and then, join me in something we both can fall into, together. For me, an ideal relationship feels like walking a tightrope between freedom and attachment—a delicate balance of maturity and mutuality. Even if our hearts aren't entirely consumed by one another, we still know how to give and receive, richly. Someone who follows their own invisible pull—like a pole drawn to a distant field—yet still weaves the everyday gently with mine. That, to me, is ideal.

This is the Relationship I Dream with Someone I Love

A Relationship Geared Toward Growth

Emotional fulfillment—being endlessly happy and joyful—is important when it comes to love. But I believe real, tangible growth matters too.

I hope for a love that feels like a staircase, one we climb together, step by step. A love where we reach out when the other is struggling, pulling each other up with strength and care. I want us to be the rope that says, "Grab on. You don't have to fall behind." I hope our love leads us toward a future that feels almost too grand to hold, the kind of future that gives us reason to grow—to become better, wiser, more beautiful versions of ourselves.

When love is healthy, I hope we both naturally begin to want to be people worthy of that love. A love that invites not just emotional depth, but meaningful evolution. A love that allows us to walk forward and say, "We've both become more whole." I want a love that keeps nudging us gently forward, always whispering: Let's go a little further. Together.

A Relationship Embracing Uneven Love

We all wish to give and receive love in equal measure—to share feelings of the same weight, where no one falls behind. But love, in its honest form, is rarely that fair.

Though I wish for an exchange of equally sized hearts, where neither falls behind, I know—perhaps too realistically—that love is never perfectly balanced. How could anyone measure their heart's depths and love with exact precision? The human heart sometimes gives more and sometimes less depending on the season. I want to have a mature relationship that understands the circumstances of those with more capacity and those with less, without letting it breed disappointment.

Since hearts, once given, are not loans but gifts, I want a relationship where we can wait patiently, even when our feelings aren't always returned in equal measure. A love where we give freely, knowing there's no guarantee of receiving the same in return. A love without calculation, without regret for what has already been given. I want to embrace love warmly—not with cold realism, but with a tempered understanding of its imperfections. After all, what's the point of keeping track of who gives more and who gives less? Love isn't about perfect balance—it's about two people finding wholeness together.

A Relationship Built to Wander Together

While everyday of love are beautiful, I long for a love where we can journey freely. I dream of a relationship where, when wearied by work and life, we can hold hands and travel to places near or far. Though we can't share every taste and preference, we can adjust to each other and walk together. To forests, trees, seas, and paths where we can focus entirely on each other, away from the noise. To waves, night skies, quiet streams, or streets at sunset.

Let's go—travel is sometimes like love itself. In those quiet, overwhelming places, love will remain as brilliant, unforgettable memories in our hearts. Those memories will be like the shimmer of light on water, beautifying our future lives. On days when we feel dulled and worn by routine, let's depart together, even without special preparations.

A Relationship
Made of Words That Stay

Is there a gift more affectionate and tender than a handwritten letter? In a letter, words dulled by familiarity are reborn, emotions take on new life. Love where letters come and go occasionally, even on ordinary days, will never grow tedious. Handwritten letters can transform ordinary days into special commemorations. I love hearts pressed firmly into paper. I value relationships with those who understand the delicacy of that act, who cherish that tenderness. Because to express love through ink and paper when spoken words fall short—that is nothing less than a blessing.

A Relationship
Woven to Hold the Whole

I want to fall into a love that cherishes, nurtures, and respects a person's entire life—not just parts of it. Since none of us are perfect and can't perfectly fulfill each other, I don't want to focus on just certain aspects when loving. So we don't fall for strengths only to turn away when seeing weaknesses. So we don't wait with specific expectations that lead to easy disappointment. Instead, I hope for a love that accepts imperfections without needing to correct them. Even if there are parts of each other we don't particularly like, we won't love—or reject—each other in fragments. Instead, we will love wholly. I want to fall into a love as wide and deep as fabric—one that wraps around an entire person, covering even the rough and angular parts, without deficiency, without hesitation.

"Love isn't something you believe in,"

"It's something you become."

Someone Who Brings 'Extra' on 'Ordinary'

Good night, sending my wishes faithfully before bed. Asking how I slept, what I dreamed, greeting the start of my day with gentle curiosity. Taking a photo of a cloudless sky to show we share the same blue above us. Mentioning wildflowers blooming beautifully along the roadside and letting me see the world through that lingering gaze. Underlining a favorite line in a beloved poetry collection and giving me as a present.

Love can be as grand as traveling to a stunning holidays, yet I especially appreciate those who understand it begins in the most ordinary moments. Someone who makes even the simplest moments feel like warmth settling into my skin Someone who asks caring questions more regularly than the moon rising each night or the sun each morning. Someone who steadily purifies my days with kind and beautiful things. Someone who underlines the words they most want to convey and shows them to me. Someone who treasures and nurtures the lukewarm tenderness we exchange daily. Someone who, though it's expected, never takes it for granted.

Love Is
Writing or Reading

Even those skilled in writing sometimes struggle to become comfortable with speed reading or understanding complex sentences. Those confident in reading may find themselves vulnerable in writing, often struggling with difficult, roundabout sentences to express their thoughts.

Similarly, I believe that giving and receiving love, while interconnected, are distinctly different domains. Just as writing and reading are separate skills, giving love and receiving it are fundamentally different processes.

Love isn't like dictation where listening and writing happen at the same time. Instead, it clearly divides into two distinct actions: reading another's heart and effectively conveying your own. Misunderstanding this mechanism of love can sometimes lead to discord—feelings of being underappreciated or growing distance.

Remember this: even when you cannot give love effectively, simply receiving it well can prevent hearts from growing cold. And some people find it difficult to receive love. Rather than feeling a wall between you, embrace their barriers and offer love unconditionally. Some find it easier to give than receive, while others excel at receiving but struggle to give. It would be wonderful if we could all do both perfectly, but where can we find perfect people or relationships? What truly matters is acknowledging the effort each person makes to guide the other. It's about striving to offer your heart in its most refined form and learning to joyfully receive your partner's efforts.

Understanding your partner's shortcomings and covering them with your strengths. Not demanding that they excel at what you do well. Faithfully fulfilling your respective roles without taking any role lightly. That's how you write each other's stories or read each other's hearts—the mechanism that won't easily fade its glow.

When We Are in Love

* Love makes us cute: I have never considered myself particularly cute, yet when I look at her, I find myself speaking in a playful, affectionate tone. Their presence alone makes me change. The more I love, the more lovable I seem to become. And because they find this version of me endearing too, we both grow tender, as if love turns us into children discovering joy for the first time. And because they, too, find this version of me endearing, we both grow tender—like children discovering joy for the first time.

* A language of our own begins to take shape, little by little. Whether it's a shortened phrase, a familiar place given a new name, a word for a certain gesture, or a term of endearment—our secret code takes shape, something only we can understand.

* We begin to resemble each other. Not in appearance, but in the way we move, the way we speak, the way we exist in the world. Love means growing alike, and perhaps it's because to love someone is, in some way, to want to become them. Maybe that's why we unconsciously begin to mirror each other, as if becoming one is the most natural thing.

* We feel a tinge of sadness sometimes. Not the kind that pulls us apart, but the kind that teaches us to meet in the middle. Disappointment isn't one-sided; it flows both ways, nudging us to understand, to adjust, to grow. Love, in its truest form, is a space where we confront our own shortcomings, where we come to know our dull edges and sharp corners. No one teaches us how to love, and yet, through love, we inevitably learn.

* We find ourselves reaching for each other's hands, often and without thinking. Not just for the warmth of touch, but because love, more than fleeting sparks, is a quiet and steady presence. It reveals itself in the simplest gestures, the way our hands seek each other, as naturally as breathing.

Besides

On a summer night, we shuffle out in slippers, laughing over the kind of stories that wouldn't make headlines—but feel like everything to us. We order late-night snacks, poke fun at our growing softness, playfully pinching at the softness we've gained, making cheerful promises—"No more midnight feasts, starting tomorrow."

In the quiet of our own little world, we become absorbed in separate hobbies, yet our presence intertwines—an invisible thread weaving us together. When we stumble upon charming little trinkets, we turn them into gifts, creating anniversaries that exist only between us.

Thus, I treasure these love stories, delicately woven into the fabric of everyday life—love that lingers, unfading. Yet, beyond all these delicate moments, the true essence of love isn't in the gestures or the days we gather. It is simply us. Us. This single word holds everything—tender, profound, and infinite. Because parting means we are no longer us, and farewell is when us dissolves into something separate. So, let us hold on to us as the most precious part of every story we write together. Nothing else matters. Us. Fragile yet infinite thing is more than enough. If we can stay close to forever in our bond, if you and I can always remain us.

My beloved, Let us love in a way where, though our expressions may differ, our hearts remain as one. Let us love with unspoken understanding, where feelings run deeper than words. Let us not love merely for each other's sake, but through each other's being. Let us not seek something beyond one another, but see each other wholly, just as we are. Let our love not blaze and burn out, but glow with quiet persistence. Rather than clinging too tightly, let us love with the quiet grace of letting go. Rather than measuring and reasoning, let us cherish with a love that is unpolished, yet true. Rather than seeking to possess, let us trust in a love that stays, even when given space to breathe. Let us build a love not adorned with illusions, but one that may seem simple—yet is honest, steadfast, and real.

Above all, let us not try to give more than our hearts can hold, nor expect more than what is freely given. Let's love-as it comes, as it goes, as freely as breath. Unbound, whole, just as it is.

Love Makes Time Where There Is None

Love should never be dismissed with the excuse of not having enough time. It is about creating moments, even when time feels scarce, making it the very center of everything. Love is not something you tend to only after everything else is finished. It is what makes you stop, what takes priority—even before the demands of the day. And it is never about forcing yourself to make time or space in your heart.

Even when there's barely room to breathe, you instinctively reach for them. You long to see their face, even if just for a moment. You need to hear their voice. Even when you know it's time to eat, you still wonder if they've eaten, feeling the urge to share your meal with them. Capturing a beautiful scene, just so you can share it with them later. And sometimes, when life feels overwhelming and your heart grows heavy, you crave them even more. To see them. To lean on them.

In love, no excuse truly holds. Did you love less, or love more? That simple difference changes everything—how much time stretches, how much space remains. Love does not offer what's left over after the day has passed. It is not about having time. It is about making time. Because you love. Because it is love. Only love creates miracles—time where none existed, space where none should be.

When Tender
Tends a Tender heart

Even knowing that giving away even a sliver of my heart would only leave me aching, I was always that naive soul—offering it anyway, just to escape the sting of the winter wind. Even knowing the hollow left behind would only deepen the more I tried to fill it, I was still that restless soul, searching for meaning in someone's words, in fleeting gestures—anything to quiet the emptiness within me.

Forgetting past wounds, bitter endings, and poor choices, I find myself drawn to someone once more—an inevitable, naive pull.

Even knowing it may hurt me, even knowing it might leave me in ruins, Today again, I hesitate—then take a step forward. I offer a piece of my heart, even as I brace for the pain.

But perhaps, love is exactly this—
The meeting of two tender hearts.

Or perhaps, it is in the meeting of two tender hearts that love is born. "Become a good person, and good people will come to you." This phrase never quite suited me. We have all been someone's not-good-enough person. And you, who reached out to me, must have been no different.

A little flawed, a little impatient, Sharp at times, carrying your own emptiness. Someone who, in trying to shine, cast shadows on those nearby.

But does it matter? Here I am, as flawed as ever, mustering the courage to step toward you. And you, imperfect and wounded, gathering your courage to step toward me.

I, with all my scars, open my heart to you—And we, though far from perfect, find ourselves drawing closer.

To the one I will love, have loved, or am loving now—Love is the meeting of one naive heart with another. Two incomplete souls, pulling each other toward an imperfect feeling. Even if we remain unfinished, even if the wounds reopen, even if the spaces within us can never be fully filled—I will not speak of endings before we even begin.

Even if others scoff and sneer, even if no one else understands, This story is ours alone to carry. The love I have known has never been defined by mere happiness or perfection.

My love, Even if all we are is two fragile hearts tending to each other, Isn't the act of reaching enough? Isn't the quiet way we become necessary to one another Reason enough to surrender, to simply be?

The Crown Belongs to Love

Do you remember?
When we lay side by side beneath a sky
So open, so vast it felt like it had been torn apart—
Watching flower petals dance on the wind,
I said, *"The petals are falling."*
But you, in a voice so soft it almost vanished into mine,
whispered: *"No, it's raining flowers."*
I could never forget that spring.
You were right, the petals weren't merely falling
—they were pouring.
No, they were not petals drift
—they were youth slipping away.

It Was All Because of Love

My anxieties, once nestled close, drift away like dandelion seeds carried by your gentle breath, only to bloom once more into a tender yellow. As if written in the stars, I knew your warmth would quiet my restless heart, yet still I found myself whispering these aches into the void of countless nights.

All of this—my trembling anxiety, my feverish longing, even these pitiful murmurs—exists only because I love you. Without care, what questions could arise? Without questions, what persistence could endure? Without persistence, what tenderness could there be? And without tenderness, what love could there be? If only you could see that all of this flows from my yearning heart. If only you could understand this heart of mine—like the night sea, deep and resonant with dark echoing with dark, resonant whispers, as if ready to embrace everything whole. If I did not love you so, could these words ever bring your face to mind, if we turned away so easily, could we call it a beautiful scene, could it be? If it folded and soaked like an umbrella, could we call it a human heart, could it be?

If my heart had not acted like a child, gently yearning despite knowing your efforts, how could you have found your way to nurture me, could it be?

All of this must be because of love, shall it be so? This heart—like an amber light, flickering both timidly and urgently, a selfish signal calling you home, shall it be so?

"Have you brought your umbrella?
It will drizzle from evening."

If only you knew how long I've been checking forecasts just to send these words.

Was Their Love Real?

Nothing harms me more than carelessly judging and measuring another's sincerity or heart. Even if feelings that were once received transform into doubt over time—wondering if they were ever genuine—I now realize it benefits me more to gracefully set aside these thoughts, assuming there were circumstances I didn't understand. When I entertain outdated suspicions—that it wasn't sincere, that they took me lightly—disrupting the past and trying to decipher feelings long gone, only the sincere heart I gave becomes pitiful. What could be more unfair to my past self, who was genuine with them at the time? If there was sincerity even for a moment, let that be enough—approach with a love that borders on maturity. Take one step closer to a love that runs even deeper.

But I understand. How painful it must have been. How many tears you must have shed revisiting that wound. You've struggled so much with your hurt.

When Spring Comes

When this winter passes and spring finally arrives, will we be able to say we love each other? Will we be able to live embracing one another? Will kisses become our everyday? Will we slip our hands under each other's bare skin and tickle? Will we become each other's tender longing?

Though I'm not someone made for warmth and lightheartedness. I've grown used to falling asleep with a frozen heart. But for you, I'll become spring. Even if we live in different seasons, I will be your spring.

You told me once that you love cherry blossoms, didn't you? Let's endure this pitiful winter just a little longer and go see the cherry blossoms together. I promise. When spring comes, let's go see the cherry blossoms. They say if you catch a falling petal, your wish comes true—I'll hold your hand and help that you catch one. Let's go see the cherry blossoms. Let's walk for a long hours, buy delicious snacks, and rest on a bench. Let's look at the moon you love so much, and if you get tired, you can lean on my shoulder—even if it's not the broadest. Let's be as quietly beautiful as any ordinary couple passing by.

Until you become my wish and I become your refuge. Let's keep going a little longer. Let's not grow distant. With our wounded hearts, let's hold each other tightly—not too soon, but not too late. When spring comes, let's promise to say we love each other. When winter passes, and spring arrives.

A Matter of the Heart

When the heart truly desires, distance is nothing—a five-hour walk feels nothing at all But when the heart is absent, even a ten-minute taxi ride feels unbearable. This is the nature of human hearts. When something matters to us, we find time for it, even while rushing breathlessly from oversleeping. But when it doesn't, we let hours slip by without a second thought. This is how desire moves within us. Is it that you're the only one who doesn't see? Even in times of war, when survival itself uncertain, love makes people hold each other close and whisper, *"Let's face the end together."* Perhaps that sounds extreme—but isn't that the depth of the human heart?

We can come up with a thousand excuses, but in the end, it is always a matter of the heart. If my heart aches with disappointment, it is simply because I was pushed aside—something else, someone else, took priority. If this happens again and again, let's stop justifying our pain.

If you can't let go just yet, then place them further away, distance them by little. And if even that feels impossible, then let yourself feel the sorrow—fully, completely. That would be better. How devastating it is to realize, too late, that you have been left at the edges—while convincing yourself you hadn't. You understand now, don't you? It was always a matter of heart. It really matters.

To You, Who Once Hurt by Love and People

I hope you meet someone who cherishes the time you give without hesitation, and the money you spend without counting. I hope you meet someone who notices the small things and says them out loud. Someone who sees these things for what they are—signs of a precious, generous heart—and says "thank you" with real sincerity.

Not someone who keeps score. Not someone who measures love by how expensive it looks.

"Thank you." "I miss you." "What did you eat today?" "The sky is so pretty tonight."

Someone who doesn't let the little things slip by, because those little things are evidence that you're always on their mind.

I hope you meet someone who decorates your days with beautiful words—not just words that sound pleasant, but words flowing from the heart. Words that make your heart home. A Voice that brings your soul to peace even if your body is far away. Affection that speaks directly, not cloaked in riddles or silence—a kind of softness that hits you straight in the heart, like a single beam of light breaking through a sky full of stormclouds.

I hope you meet not someone who perfectly matches your ideal type, but someone who matches less than expected, yet gradually becomes your world. Someone with whom time spent together approaches the ideal. Someone who makes compromise feel natural, not forced. Someone whose differences, instead of creating distance, leave space for wildflowers to bloom. Someone whose flaws make you want to apply healing balm again and again. In such a heart, love settles more deeply.

To everyone reading this, I wish for such relationships to be with you.

"What does it mean to forget something?"

"To remember it over and over until, one day, you no longer even think about forgetting."

Perhaps It Wasn't Love

It wasn't my love that made them happy—it was their own gentle heart, full of love for me. When I embraced them, it wasn't my warmth they felt—it was the warmth of their own love, reflected back. They said I made them happy, but in truth, I had given them nothing at all. Their love circled back to them like a boomerang, shaping their own happiness. What I cherished wasn't them, but their tireless heart, always so kind to me. Whether they realized it or not, I grew weary of a love that never paused to catch its breath.

In the end, I had no choice but to shatter the happiness we built. I told myself it wasn't the kind of happiness that could last. I clung to shallow excuses as I walked away—telling myself we deserved a love that felt right, that we should each find our way to something better.

People often mistake what it is that truly brings them happiness. Sometimes, love only becomes clear in hindsight—"Ah, so that was love." Other times, we find ourselves wondering, "Perhaps it was never love at all."

And maybe, just maybe, it was never love to begin with.

Reasons for Breakups
That Now Make Sense

Too Much Know
Comes to the End

Some relationships come to the end since they know too much each other.

The more intimately we discovered every detail about each other, ironically, the less space remained for new discoveries, until we found ourselves feeling like strangers bound by overwhelming familiarity. Does knowing someone completely mean we can no longer truly see them?

Each person holds something like a password to their heart, and sometimes we know it so well that we can no longer see it clearly. It's like a door lock combination worn down from pressing the same digits too many times. The numbers are still there, but they've faded into a blur.

And that's when we find ourselves at the threshold of a past we can never step into again.

We kept meeting, but only out of habit. But somewhere along the line, we forgot those once-cherished moments, forgotten dates and numbers, forgotten vows and promises—everything that once carried so much meaning.

Because we loved feverishly. Because we depended on and leaned on each other. Because we held deep expectations.

Because we repeated it, over and over, letting each other in. Because we let hatred and resentment in as well.

In the end, our breakup was so inevitable, we could see it even with our eyes closed.

When You Can't Envision a Future Together

Some relationships are warm, loving, and full of joy—yet the future refuses to take shape. We struggle between our immediate emotions and our hopes for tomorrow, eventually deciding to let go for the sake of something more stable. We may not fully understand what we yearned for or expected, but we know this: the future with them remained stubbornly unclear.

In the end, love carries a longing too deep to be satisfied by fleeting warmth alone.

Different Blooming Seasons in Love

Some love stories don't fail because of who we are or how we feel—but simply because the timing is wrong. It was love that never had the chance to bloom—one that, in hindsight, belonged to a fleeting spring.

Maybe we were still healing from past wounds. Or maybe life pulled us in opposite directions, making our love feel like mismatched puzzle pieces. It was both heartbreaking and achingly beautiful at once.

There's always one person we couldn't keep, simply because time wasn't on our side—the one we think of now and then, like cherry blossoms that fell before spring had the chance to settle in.

When Love for the Person Grows Beyond Romance

I used to think it was a lie when people said they broke up because they loved too much, but over time, I've come to understand. Perhaps it's because we cherished them more as a someone than as a lover. We still want to treasure them and stay by their side, yet there are things we simply can't give—promises about the future, meeting as often as we'd like, the gifts we'd hoped to offer, or days free of emotional tension. The gap between what we want to give and what we actually can becomes too wide to ignore.

It starts to feel as though keeping them close might only diminish their life. Even this thought can feel like an excuse, tangled up in complicated emotions that pass through our hearts. And so, sometimes, we leave—knowing full well we'll regret it. Just once in a lifetime, there's someone we let go of because we saw how exhausting the process would be, how inevitable the outcome—someone we loved with the profound tenderness of simply being ourselves.

What If

"Please don't go.", "Don't be happy without me.", "It hurts like hell.", "Let's try again.", "Let's not do this.", "Let's go together."... those are the things I should've said. But instead, I told him, "Let's be happy," "Let's both live well," and ended it. I thought that was what mature love looked like. I thought that was how adults let go. I swallowed countless sentences that threatened to burst from my mouth. Maybe she's doing well. Maybe I'm supposed to be, too. But I still carry those soft, aching what-ifs. If I had broken down just once—What if I had begged, what if I had reached out with my whole heart, what if I had found the courage to ask her to stay—Would we still be traveling the world together, promising each other forever? Would I still be able to tell you "beautiful" while watching the sunset?

And So, Love Comes

There are those who, when they begin to hold someone in their heart, feel the urge to run—despite wanting nothing more than to stay by their side. People who, after walking beside someone for too long, lose the ability to walk alone. People who, once accustomed to sharing meals with someone across the table, suddenly find the thought of eating alone terrifying.

Some people, more familiar with the nausea of instability than the comfort of long-settled stillness, push others away and quietly bear their own sorrow. Some blurt out words they don't mean, choosing to shoulder both the wounds and the sorrow, may seem like they're avoiding love, their fears stemming from deep scars—or from having once left a wound too deep in someone else. But in truth, they are those who are deeply sincere about love, standing in the middle of their own relentless pursuit of it.

To the outside world, they may seem broken. But in truth, they are closer to normal—because they have never wasted love on something undeserving. Like a broken compass, it's hard to find direction, when it comes to love, their gaze never strays.

I stand with the love of people like them. I've come to understand that love isn't always bathed in light and joy. Perhaps love is closer to sorrow—dense and heavy, like deep, sinking mud. Still, I would stand like a candle, trembling in the wind yet refusing to die out—melting my tears into wax, melting into tears that harden into wax, only to fuel the light that brightens my love.

But please, do not let yourself be swallowed by that dark tide. Do not wear yourself away, believing your feelings are worthless or wrong.

"Even so, love draws near."

No— *"Love draws near because of it all."*

And so, love comes quietly—but never fails to stay.

To My Beloved Mother

Mom Still Thinks of Me

I'm the kind of person who thinks earning is more important than spending, so my approach to money is different from most. "Money can always be earned again," I often tell myself, indulging in extravagance without a second thought. But my mother is different, She has tasted nothing but poverty throughout my childhood and until I was able to stand on my own, and for her, life has always felt more like a fleeting illusion than a settled home.

To her, careful spending wasn't just a habit—it was a necessity. She always worries about my spending habits. "Son, earning well is important, but you must spend wisely," she says, adding various other pieces of advice. Each time, I think to myself, 'Mom, wise spending requires time and thought—that's a waste of resources for me. I'd rather spend thoughtlessly and invest my time elsewhere.' Yet, in those moments, I take her small hand in mine and ask anyway: "Mom, something happened the other day—should I buy this or not?"

We all feel valued when someone seeks our advice, when our words matter to another. I want my mother to feel the weight of her own significance. Though our opinions and lifestyles differ, I nod in agreement with her words and frequently ask,

"What would you do in this situation, Mom?" or "Mom, is this the right way to do it?" Often, I already know the answers to these questions. They carry the hidden message: "I am still growing in the palm of your hand."

When I see myself still growing beside her, I hope her life, too, can remain forever youthful. Mom, you are still raising me, just as you always have. I still need you. I want to keep growing wisely, with you by my side. This time, I don't ask—I answer.

Even past thirty, I still find myself calling for my mother over the smallest things. It's not about being needy—I know that even as she moves with seeming annoyance, deep down, she's smiling. With time, we become more aware of what it means to be needed. Even as I grow older, I want to remain someone worth calling for. When I reach middle age, I hope to be someone still necessary to those I cherish, just like my mother. Though I might grumble and pretend indifference, in my heart, I'll quietly hope—to be someone they call for, even in the smallest moments. Perhaps this alone is enough to say we have lived well.

To Be Called by Name, Like Her

Even now, well into my thirties, I still catch myself calling out for my mom over the smallest things. Not out of neediness—just knowing she'll sigh, pretend she's annoyed, and still come... smiling on the inside. As time goes on, we become more aware of their own usefulness. Even as I grow worn, I hope to remain needed. When I reach that age of steadiness—what they call the age of not being shaken—I want to be like my mother: Someone still worth calling for, someone still instinctively turned to. And even if I grumble, even if I act like I don't care, in my heart, I'll be hoping the same—to be a name someone still looks for, even for things that don't matter much.

Maybe that alone means we've lived well.
Maybe that's all we ever really needed—to live well.

Rice Tinted with Fish

When I think of my mother, I think of fish. My father and I both leaned more toward meat, but my mother grew up in a small port town famed for its pungent salted seafood, *"jeotgal"*. Because of that, the briny smell of fish and all kinds of fermented sea flavors were part of her childhood and youth, anchoring her tastes firmly.

Whenever we travel together or go out on a simple "date," I'll ask, "Mom, what do you feel like eating?" and nine times out of ten, she'll say she wants fish or seafood. It might just be grilled mackerel, but after a lifetime of holding back, she now cleans every last bit of it with expert precision.

My mother is quite petite. She does eat heartily for her size, but being small, she never manages to finish all her rice. By the end of a meal, there's always an endearing amount left in her bowl, and that's when I swoop in and eat it. Each time, she insists it's dirty and tries to stop me, but I do it anyway. Normally,

I'm the type who can't stand sharing a straw, or slurping soup that someone else's spoon has dipped into. Yet with my mom's leftover rice, I feel no hesitation.

There's something about that rice she leaves behind—the hint of fish lingering in each grain, the tiny scraps of flesh still clinging, and the faint smear of jeotgal seasoning—that I find oddly delightful. Mom may call it "dirty," but nothing she leaves behind feels dirty to me. It simply makes sense that it wouldn't. It has to be that way.

If I were to feel disgust at the food of the very person who's cared for me all my life—could I claim to be thinking straight? It would make me less than an animal; even baby animals lick their parents' fur in affection.

My parents gifted me the life I have now. Surely it's only right that I accept, without hesitation, whatever remains of theirs—even if it's just a few grains of fish-tinted rice.

The Taste of My Mother's Stew

I've always loved my mother's soybean paste stew. She cooks it until the chunks are so soft they practically melt. Personally, I prefer a version that still has a bit of bite—like the fresh pot you'd get in a restaurant. But I know hers has been simmered again and again, on the stove far longer than any restaurant would allow. Mom starts early, expecting me to arrive, keeping it warm just in case. If I'm late, she turns off the heat, then fires it up again once I finally come. The zucchini, potato, and tofu—once firm—have collapsed under the weight of waiting, soft, wrinkled, and tender.

I wish I could freeze my mother's clock right here. Even now, well into my thirties, I often find myself tearing up at the dinner table.

Ms. Lilac Kim

I can't quite recall our very first meeting. All I really know about that moment is that she was the one who hoped I'd keep breathing when I entered this world—naked, still slick with amniotic fluid. That's it. I came into being through her pain and endurance, and through her, I first saw and experienced the world. These days, she's small enough to fit snugly in my arms, but back when I was little, she was so big to me that I could run around on her palm as if it were an entire playground—a tall fence that enclosed my whole world.

One day, while writing about my mother, I grew curious about the word "Mom." I noticed that in many languages, people use simple syllables like "mama," so I wondered if "Mom" might be one of the easiest words to say in Korean as well—like a natural sound you make just by opening and closing your mouth: "m-o-m." Maybe it's because "Mom" is often the very first word a baby learns to speak. I imagined a time when language itself formed around what was easiest for a newborn mouth to say.

At some point, though, I started feeling a tinge of regret about how simple that word is. We each live life under our own names, but a mother's name can disappear so easily from the world, just like that—poof. It's a precious change that occurs when she becomes someone's mother, yet it also marks a new life where she is given so little recognition as herself.

Before you know it, people are calling her "the mother of me and my sister." She's "Honey" or "You" to my dad. She's "Mom" or "Mother" to me. As life goes on, all sorts of new titles pop up to replace her real name—Kim Jiyoung, and eventually Lilac Kim. Each time, she took these names for granted, adapting as if it were perfectly natural, and her original name and life slowly wore away, bit by bit.

Ever since I was born, Mom lived every day, every year, every decade, losing a little piece of herself. Instead of the seafood she loved, she made the pork belly the family preferred. Instead of the pink dress she wanted, she spent money on my extracurricular worksheets. Instead of the dream trip to Jeju Island, she sent me on my school trip. Instead of buying the house she wanted, she saved to put me through college. Over the years, she was hounded by the demands of sacrifice and postponement, leaving her own wishes behind.

In truth, "Lilac Kim" is a name she chose for herself later in life. For the first half of her life, she lived as Kim Jiyoung. A few years ago, she must have felt I'd finally outgrown her palm, because she started leaning on me in ways she never had before. In the process, it seemed like she was trying to reclaim the life she'd set aside. Like squeezing the very last bit of toothpaste from a flattened tube to brush her yellowed teeth—she was squeezing out the remnants of a life she once used up, trying to scrub away the years that had gone dull.

That first big step was changing her name to one she'd always dreamed of having: Lilac Kim. She even reissued her ID card. She used to say "Kim Jiyoung" sounded too old-fashioned, and she'd always hoped to rename herself someday. Only now did that wish come true. Afterward, she began filling in the missing puzzle pieces of her half-finished life, crossing off small items from a bucket list. For instance, she's been focusing on her health, which she'd neglected for most of her life, and going to church gatherings to rediscover the joy of meeting people. Sometimes she buys the clothes she actually wants, or picks up a new instrument to learn—nothing earth-shattering, but she's recovering those small things she once lost. Transitioning from "Mom," to Kim Jiyoung, and finally to Lilac Kim. I want to cheer on every step of that metamorphosis.

Maybe "Mom" is the easiest word in the world. It's probably the first word we come to know—a person and a memory so familiar that we say it without thinking, all our lives. "Mom." Because of that, I worry we take it for granted, letting it slip casually from our tongues, never once pausing to think about her real name and life. As for me, I'd like to bring back the names "Kim Jiyoung" and "Lilac Kim," the ones she lost somewhere along the way. I want to say them out loud, to call her "Jiyoung," "Lilac," like it's the most natural thing—something affectionate and dear. Our dear Jiyoung, our bright Lilac. Cute, lovely Ms. Lilac Kim. Little by little, I hope it reminds her of the life she once let fade away. I confess, I'm afraid of her growing old too quickly. I feel an urgent need to help her remember who she is—yet I don't want to rush, for fear of breaking her. Like I'm gently coaxing her forward.

As she ages, I sometimes think about dementia. Maybe, I tell myself, people get dementia before death as a way to forget the terror of dying. Whenever that thought crosses my mind, the sadness and fear I feel about what might happen to Mom and me is overwhelming. There's no promise it won't happen to her. Yet still, I try to be brave and reason: "If death is that frightening, maybe forgetting is a relief." It's tragic, but at the same time, perhaps it's less painful to forget. Even so, I have one small hope: that if we end up forgetting most of our lives, we don't forget each other's names. If my mother ever develops dementia, I hope she remembers who she is—Lilac Kim—and who I am. If I ever lose my memory, I hope the names "Lilac Kim" and "Mom" stay with me, so that someday, should we both find ourselves in that place beyond, we can search for each other like two old friends who never lost touch.

Before it's too late, I want to help her rediscover all the parts of Kim Jiyoung and Lilac Kim she might have lost in the corners of her life. I want her to remember herself for as long as possible, never forgetting her own name. Even if I'm a little late, I still want to make sure it's not too late.

IV

Stand Your Ground

Filling My Life With Things I Love

The more we surround ourselves with what we love, the more naturally our lives grow rich. These cherished things wash away the dust that settles thick upon our days, keeping our emotions clear and untainted, even amid accumulating negative feelings. I know now—when surrounded by things I love, I need not chase after impossible happiness to find peace in my days, nor measure my success against anything but my own heart. A dress in my favorite color, a blanket with just the right roughness against my skin, incense sticks that release a fragrance I want to keep close, poetry books resting beside me, their pages revisited time and time again. But they need not be objects at all—a birthday card written in my loving mother's hand, encouraging messages from friends, and the New Year's resolutions I once made with determination. Filling my space with things I love. Choosing to dwell where gentleness lingers in my sight. Never forgetting the promises I've made to myself. Time and space filled with things I cherish by my own measure support me through anything, keeping me unshaken. I will thoughtfully gather the things I long to see, to touch, to hear—pieces of beauty, fragments of warmth. And so, becoming someone who knows how to spend days as luminous and rich as sunlight shimmering on water. I wish to offer only the purest kindness to those I love.

My dear, I get older, I find I can't live without supplements anymore. That's why I'm telling you this—nourish yourself well while you're young. It's not about taking medicine only when you're sick. Like me, if you don't take care of yourself now, you'll find it harder when you're older. I mean this with all my heart—when you're healthy and full of energy, that's when you should look after your body.

Promise me, always ask me before you buy any supplements. No matter how good something may seem, it's useless if your body can't absorb it well. Did you know that Vitamin D needs to be taken with calcium to be effective? Keep this in mind, my son. Don't just consume things blindly because you hear they're beneficial. Your mother didn't know these things and spent her whole life foolishly, only taking medicine on the surface. What truly matters is how well your body—and your heart—can receive and take things in. That's the most important thing. Do you understand what I'm saying?

My beloved dear, please take good care of yourself.

- Words from my mother, as she handed me supplements -

What Matters Most Is Steadfast Authenticity

I believe the secret to sustaining a flexible life lies not in sudden success, nor in wisdom earned through repeated trials, nor even in the support of many around us. What matters most is steadfast authenticity. Though we may waver, swayed by the endless rise and fall of life, what truly holds us together is the grace to remain true to ourselves, as we always have before.

It is the quiet resolve to step away briefly, yet find our way back—effortlessly, as if we had never strayed. It is remembering, always, through the relentless motion of life, the direction that is truly ours. Like a quiet instinct, it is the pull that draws us inward, even after we have momentarily drifted. For if we lose ourselves, no success, no time, no relationship will matter. When we lose ourselves, the precious things we hold become not truly ours—they become merely the fruits of chasing empty shells. Life becomes most fragile, most prone to crumbling, when we are not ourselves.

Even if we falter, even if we lag behind, our hearts must remain steady—always returning to who we are.

"What matters most is steadfast authenticity."

Each of us carries our own universe above,

and cradles an ocean within our hearts.

Beneath our feet stretches a wilderness unknown to others,

while at the tip of our nose,

a secret garden blooms in silence.

At our fingertips, butterflies flutter—

seen only by us.

Behind us, we long for shadows

whose names we alone remember.

Within each of us, a universe unfolds—

one that no other can truly know.

Preserving My Whole Self

Being Alone Can Be Enough

While a life forced into solitude breeds loneliness, a life that embraces solitude makes us more whole, more colorful. To feel at ease alone, I create small joys just for myself. I prepare little delights for each season, and lay down reasons to look forward to my weekends.

The important thing is that these joys are not contingent on anyone else—
they must be pleasures I can savor on my own. An escape from exhausting routines and wearying relationships doesn't always require a grand journey or lavish spending.

If we can lay down our burdens and find even the smallest joy in solitude, then without grand journeys or indulgences, it is more than enough. Breaking free from exhausting routines and relationships doesn't always require grand journeys or indulgence. If we can set down our mental burdens and find joy in solitude, that alone is enough—no journey or purchase needed.

Work That Satisfies
Money That Sustains

I work diligently to create financial breathing room. When I can make my immediate world abundant enough to feel content, and when I can honestly say I've been diligent in my work, then I can stand tall against any criticism or mistake.

Satisfaction in one's work is like a medal of honor in life, raising the most fundamental pride we can possess.

For Today, I Choose to Rest

The ability to fall asleep by turning off unnecessary thoughts is one of life's quiet blessings. Even if it doesn't come easily, what matters is choosing a life that leans in that direction. In the middle of swirling anxieties, being able to say, "Let tomorrow's me figure it out," and flipping the switch in your mind—that, too, is a form of self-care. Using less energy today lets you give more tomorrow. After all, rest is not indulgence; it's an investment in your future. Needless worries only cloud the clarity of tomorrow.

Deep Understanding and
Acceptance of Myself

I try to be honest with the emotions that live in me. People are surprisingly good at lying to themselves, so I try to place a mirror inside my mind and look at myself clearly. Especially the parts I usually avoid: insecurities, unwarranted shame, victimhood. Even if I pretend they don't exist on the surface, I keep asking myself questions—patiently, gently—so that I can acknowledge their presence. Before I can turn these negative sprouts into something useful, I must first pass through the process of understanding and accepting them. Especially the things I want to hide—feelings of inferiority, excessive self-doubt, and victim mentality—I really try to face them all.

Putting My Promises to Myself First

I firmly decline appointments that feel unnecessary. Few things are as exhausting as meeting someone when we have no energy to spare. Unless I truly want to see them, have much to share, or have clear purpose in meeting, I absolutely refrain from appointments that might spiral into stress. If a relationship would wither from missing one meeting, what could be more pointless? When life gets busy and time grows scarce, sometimes we need a period of quietly tending only to our own days.

I Made It

Looking back on the years gone by, I don't think it was painful words that shaped my growth. Nor was it the series of events that nearly broke me. Nor the enduring times of perseverance. To be precise, growth was possible because there was a version of myself that reluctantly changed through countless catalysts. In the end, I've grown not by the grace of wounds or time, but by my own determination to change.

So I hope those reading this won't get hurt unnecessarily. I hope they won't suffer for extended periods. I hope they won't push themselves to the edge thinking, "This pain will help me grow." I hope they won't create justifications to easily allow future wounds. Because it wasn't thanks to painful wounds and difficult times that you grew—it was because you yourself sought opportunities for growth and reluctantly changed.

Not all wounds become catalysts for growth. There are things that countless hours cannot resolve. So I hope your future life won't be one where you rationalize wounds as reasons for growth, permitting them too easily. I hope you'll distance yourself from a life that casually diminishes your achievements by saying time solved everything.

Looking back on the years that have passed, I don't believe it was painful words that shaped my growth. Nor was it the series of events that almost broke me. Nor the enduring periods of perseverance. To be precise, growth came because there was a version of myself that reluctantly changed through countless catalysts. In the end, I grew not through the grace of wounds or time, but by my own determination to change.

So I hope those reading this won't get hurt unnecessarily. I hope they won't suffer for long periods. I hope they won't push themselves to the edge thinking, "This pain will help me grow." I hope they won't create justifications that allow future wounds too easily. Because it wasn't thanks to painful wounds and difficult times that you grew—it was because you yourself sought opportunities for growth and reluctantly changed.

Not all wounds become catalysts for growth. Some things countless hours can't be resolved. So, I hope your future won't be one where you rationalize wounds as reasons for growth, allowing them too easily. I hope you'll distance yourself from a life that casually diminishes your achievements by claiming the time solved everything.

Dear My Greatest Enemy

"I am the greatest enemy my own, for no one makes me suffer more than I do myself."

These are the words I once scribbled in my notebook when my world was shaking, when I felt myself breaking.

Looking back, I see the truth in them. I have been always the one makes life the hardest, yet I am also the one who can bring myself the most happiness.

If I am struggling, it is mostly because of me,
and if I am happy, I owe it largely to myself.
If I have suffered, it was mostly because of me,
and if I have been happy, I owed it largely to myself.

Nothing could wound me without my permission.
Nothing could bring me joy without my presence.

The emotions I carry are born within me, shaping the course of my life. Every consequence I face is, in one way or another, the result of my own choices.

So when I struggle with burdens I should not bear,
when I torment myself over things beyond my control,
I know the fault is mine alone.

Because standing in my way, always, is my greatest enemy—myself.

The one who clings out of fear.
The one who refuses to let go, only to drown in regret.
The one who tries to change what cannot be changed,
who knowingly steps into storms that could have been avoided.

There was no one else to blame.

And yet, I searched for something—someone—to point my finger at. But in the end, the only shadow beside me was my own.

Even when I know this truth, I still struggle to stop the cycle. And in those moments, I must remember:

Worry only for what is truly worth worrying about.
Struggle only for what is worth the fight.

There is a limit to the emotions and energy I can pour out.
Resting my heart is not a weakness—it is the most productive thing I can do.

Let go fully of what is meant to be released.
Hold close and grieve only what is worth regretting.

The world does not end with one storm.
It only darkens for a while—
And after the rain, the sky will clear again.

So do not turn yourself into too great an enemy.

For though I have made myself my own worst foe,
I must remember—
Before I was ever my greatest enemy,
I was my own closest friend.

A Reason to Love Myself

I wonder—Have I ever loved myself with the same fever-like intensity I've felt for others?

To like and accept myself is more precious than any love this world could offer.

It is the most valuable, the most beautiful—the greatest kindness, irreplaceable in its meaning.

And if you cannot find reasons to love yourself, remember this:

'Right now' is always the perfect time to love who you are.

To seek reasons to cherish yourself, even if just for this moment, is a luxury we too often overlook.

Shape of Myself

When my heart turns toward myself, I find stability that nothing else can replace. A wholeness that stands on its own, needing no external support to endure. The quiet serenity of knowing how to rely on myself.

On days when I feel less radiant, I remind myself—it's not that I lack beauty, but that the world around me is shining brightly. Knowing how to reject both unnecessary interference and self-doubt. Knowing how to stay anchored in my heart, even as life's waves rise, and the winds grow fierce. Having a heart that may sway but never shatter, and eyes that will not drown in sorrow. Being myself— both the hardest and most freeing path to the life I wish to live.

However, therefore, nevertheless
—a life that remains true to who I am.

How beautiful yet precarious this way of living is.

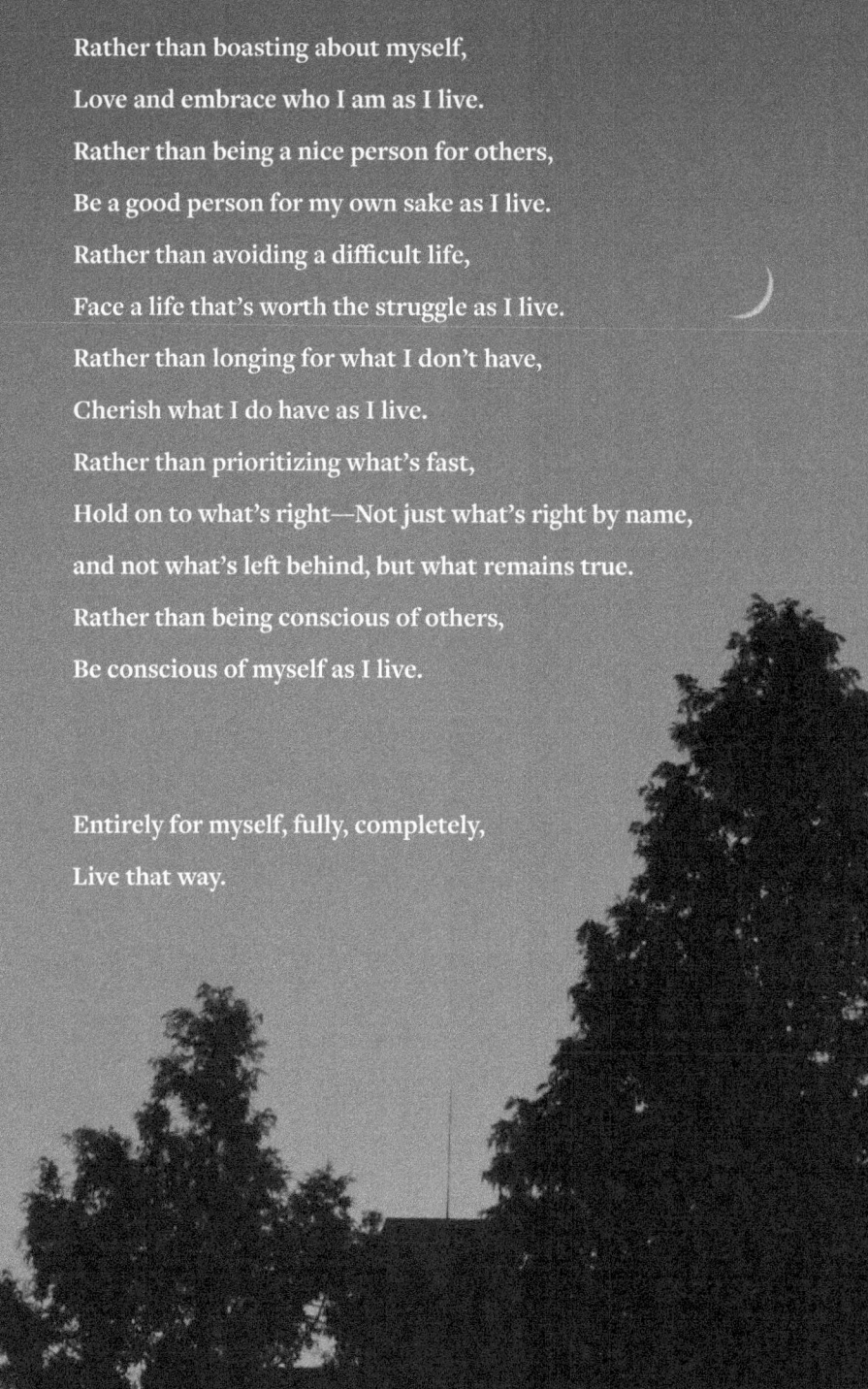

Rather than boasting about myself,

Love and embrace who I am as I live.

Rather than being a nice person for others,

Be a good person for my own sake as I live.

Rather than avoiding a difficult life,

Face a life that's worth the struggle as I live.

Rather than longing for what I don't have,

Cherish what I do have as I live.

Rather than prioritizing what's fast,

Hold on to what's right—Not just what's right by name,

and not what's left behind, but what remains true.

Rather than being conscious of others,

Be conscious of myself as I live.

Entirely for myself, fully, completely,

Live that way.

On Loving Oneself

Knowing Oneself

To love oneself does not simply mean embracing and comforting oneself. Rather, I believe it means knowing oneself most intimately. It is understanding when to be gentle and when to push forward. On a simple level, it is recognizing the spaces that brings us ease and the stories that ignite our curiosity on a deeper level, it is understanding where we flourish, what kind of people we are drawn to—or wish to avoid. More profoundly, it is understanding. our true strengths and weaknesses, knowing what shapes our values in life. It is learning from the things we might otherwise overlook, acknowledging our flaws in the very places we'd rather ignore. For love, in its purest form, is complete and intimate knowing.

Not All Confidence Is Love

High self-esteem does not automatically equate to self-love. An abundance of confidence does not inherently mean true self-care. While self-love may naturally lead to confidence and self-esteem, the reverse is not always true. Confidence and self-esteem, when not rooted in true self-awareness, can leave us vulnerable— easily shaken by the world. A belief that does not come from within—one without foundation— can turn into an irreparable regret.

The Courtesy I Owe Myself

We make an effort to show respect and recognition to others, yet often fail to extend the same courtesy to ourselves. Disrespecting oneself stems from a lack of self-trust. Honoring oneself begins with believing in one's own worth. This is not about blind confidence. There will be moments when, without exception, we must trust ourselves. For if we cannot believe in ourselves, who else will?

Centered, Not Closed

Living an independent and self-directed life does not mean excluding others or thinking only of oneself. It means being aware of the world around us, while keeping ourselves at the center. When misunderstood, this balance can easily slip into selfishness. Think of it as reading comments on a post we have written. Some responses may challenge our viewpoint— being self-directed does not mean ignoring them, but rather examining them with curiosity, learning from what is worth learning. Yet, we also have the right to filter out what does not align with us. We can cherish the words that inspire us, allow them to push us toward growth. And we can reread our own words, finding pride in them, too. This is what it means to live with both autonomy and openness.

Proud, Without Proof

Let's consider the definition of confidence:

"*A feeling of self-assurance.*" A feeling—a state of mind, not something we must earn through great accomplishments. Self-acceptance and conviction in our own existence do not require grand achievements. Let's grant ourselves this acceptance. We can be proud of ourselves, even when we have achieved nothing extraordinary. Finding pride in the smallest things— in the quiet, ordinary moments—becomes the very essence that makes life richer. We must first take pride in ourselves before we can truly take pride in what we do. We must be proud of ourselves before we can genuinely celebrate the accomplishments of others.

Sentence Somewhere That Lifts You Up

From the time I was five to eight, perhaps—"Come home before it's late." These were the words my grandmother often said as she prepared stir-fried mushrooms from those we picked in the hills behind our house or fish cake soup from the ones bought at the central market. Come back before it gets too late, she'd say. Come home for dinner before sunset. Though I don't remember everything clearly, I hold onto the tenderness of those days and make a quiet promise to myself.

I keep on living. Just as she said, when waves of nameless loneliness wash over me, I try to leap toward the peace of knowing—I, too, have a place to return to, a place where I belong. If inexplicable sorrow threatens to break me, I remind myself: we all have somewhere we must enter, someone we are meant to return to. We are all tied to places and relationships that hold us steady.

Even when we find ourselves sitting in the cold wind, crying without purpose, we remain the ones destined to return—to warm dinner tables, to arms that have been waiting, to be someone's hope, someone's quiet warmth, the irreplaceable presence in a heart that holds us dear, bound by tenderness, impossible not to love.

"Come home before it's late."

In life, each of us carries at least one sentence that, in its own way, lifts us up. That sentence—will carry us as always.

Can We Love Without Blaming?

There are two paradoxical keys to sustaining a relationship: finding ways to be happy together, and finding ways to struggle with each other.

Ironically, the more we treasure something, the more conflict seems to creep in, casting a shadow over harmony This is because we are in the process of becoming one. Expectations arise. Promises form. And within them, disappointment and resentment take root. Two people, once free to move at their own pace, now find themselves bound together—walking a three-legged race, trying to synchronize their steps through days, months, years. Naturally, there will be friction, missteps, and wounds that reopen time and again.

That is why I believe the key to sustaining a precious relationship lies not in how we fulfill each other, but in how we endure each other's criticism. The deeper the love, the more inevitable this truth becomes. How do we let resentment sharpen our awareness without letting it tear us apart? In the storm of emotions—jealousy, inferiority, longing—how do we give our negativity a shape that does not destroy? Love cannot survive on silent endurance and one-sided sacrifice alone. To last, we must ask ourselves: how do we wound without breaking?

Relationships are like tendons— what matters is not how far they stretch, but how they contract and hold tension. It is in that tension, in the ability to tighten and withstand strain, that real connection forms. True connection isn't found in ease, but in the ability to tighten, hold, and endure tension without snapping. Only by learning this balance can we hold each other tightly enough—not to suffocate, but to make sure that even when we fall, we fall together.

If we turn inward, we find another layer of relationship:not the one between self and others,but the one we hold with ourselves, relentless and inescapable.

To love oneself is to exist in a constant battle—between light and shadow, between hope and despair. The self that reaches to the sun and the self that lingers in darkness are bound together, each insisting on its own pace, each struggling to steer the same path. each stubbornly moving at its own pace, each struggling to guide the same path Thus, even in our relationship with ourselves, the same two questions remain: how do we seek happiness, and how do we struggle with ourselves? And so, even within ourselves, the same two questions persist: how do we find happiness, and how do we endure our own struggles?

The words we use to define relationships—"love," "friendship," "connection," "fate"—are soft in sound, gentle in tone. Many believe that within them lies only harmony, peace, and stability. But love is a battlefield. Connection is friction. To stay close to someone is to brush against their edges—sometimes gently, sometimes painfully

That is why, to truly love ourselves, we must be willing to battle ourselves. This is not about compromise—it is about confrontation. Within the chasm between light and dark, how do we challenge ourselves? What parts of us must we cast away? What must we allow to die? How do we push ourselves forward? How do we fight ourselves, again and again?

Thus, the path to self-love is paved with self-reproach. We must fight—fight for the past selves we abandoned, for the present selves we question, for the future selves we have yet to become.

We have all done something wrong. Even if the world never sees it, we carry our sins in the shadows of our hearts. How do we make amends? Do we justify our selfishness, or do we refuse to accept what cannot be excused?

Everyone makes mistakes. Some skillfully shift the blame onto others, while others step forward to accept their faults, even when it costs them dearly. When others criticize us for our missteps, will it break us—or will it make us stronger? To make the right choices, we must fight. Through what battles, through what self-reckoning, will we keep from repeating our missteps?

Everyone feels inferior at times. Sometimes, that inferiority festers into quiet resentment. Other times, it spills into arrogance, too large for the vessel that holds it. And sometimes, it manifests as imitation—a desperate attempt to mirror the very thing we envy. Among these tangled emotions, how do we hold ourselves accountable? Do we raise the whip against our own weaknesses?

Love is such a painful thing. At its core, every relationship is a struggle. Connection means enduring wounds. Harmony is a balance of mutual reproach. Peace is a delicate act of maintaining tension. In our relationship with ourselves, the path to self-love is not paved by soothing praise or gentle acceptance alone—but must be preceded by anguish, estrangement, and the uncompromising act of confronting and reproaching the self.

How could I ever embrace this flawed self without judgment?
How could I carry this sharp-edged life without feeling its pain?

My dear, I hope you'll quit smoking and drink only in moderation. Please eat well, even if it feels like a hassle, with the side dishes I send. And no matter how busy life gets, always make time to exercise. Once health is lost, everything else crumbles. Take care of yourself.

No achievement, no ambition is worth sacrificing your precious body. No goal is worth clinging to, no person worth holding on to, if it means breaking yourself in the process. No one in this world is worth resenting if it comes at the cost of your well-being.

You are the most precious thing in this world. No matter where you look, more valuable than you. So don't wear yourself down, and don't treat yourself carelessly. Without your health, nothing else truly matters.
Here I go again, nagging as always. But you understand your mother's heart, don't you, my son?

- My mother's words of advice, calling me out of the blue for no particular reason -

The Courage to Give Up

It takes courage to let things fall apart. Running backward requires as much strength as running forward. While building a structure demands tremendous effort, tearing it down can be equally taxing.

In fact, sometimes falling apart feels more difficult than standing up. Often, we rise again because we lack the strength to collapse fully. Because we feel ashamed of ourselves. Because it feels like betraying our own efforts. Because it makes us feel inadequate. Because we fear we might never stand again. Some days, the reaction of others frightens us more than our own struggles. We fear being pointed at. We dread the whispers about us. We feel like we're betraying those who believed in us. And then, we worry they'll never trust us again. That we'll end up alone.

So even when we know we should stop, we cannot find the strength to let things crumble. We lack courage. Because we've only been taught how to win, how to persevere. Because we've only learned how to build, considering forward movement as the only right answer. Because anything opposite to this feels wrong. So, when we do fall apart, when we do look backward, our first instinct is to hide it from others.

To my past self who thought this way, to you who might be thinking this way now, I want to say: There is nothing wrong with letting go. You no longer need to hide it.

I applaud you. Whether you collapsed yesterday, today, a year ago, or will collapse a year from now, I send applause, not accusation, to everything that's falling apart. For showing true courage. For enduring such difficulty. For doing the right thing. For facing one of life's greatest challenges.

And I wish for you: May your journey back reveal beautiful scenery you missed while running forward. May there be side paths leading you to unexpected destinations. May you continue running steadily on these new paths. May a more solid structure rise from the ruins of your fallen efforts—not necessarily taller, but one that embodies the beautiful dreams you've held. Even if everything collapses, as long as your core self remains intact, you can reach new places and build again. So, I applaud you who won't crumble in the battle with yourself. I applaud you who won't be defeated. And I applaud your courage to let go of something, your decision to surrender something.

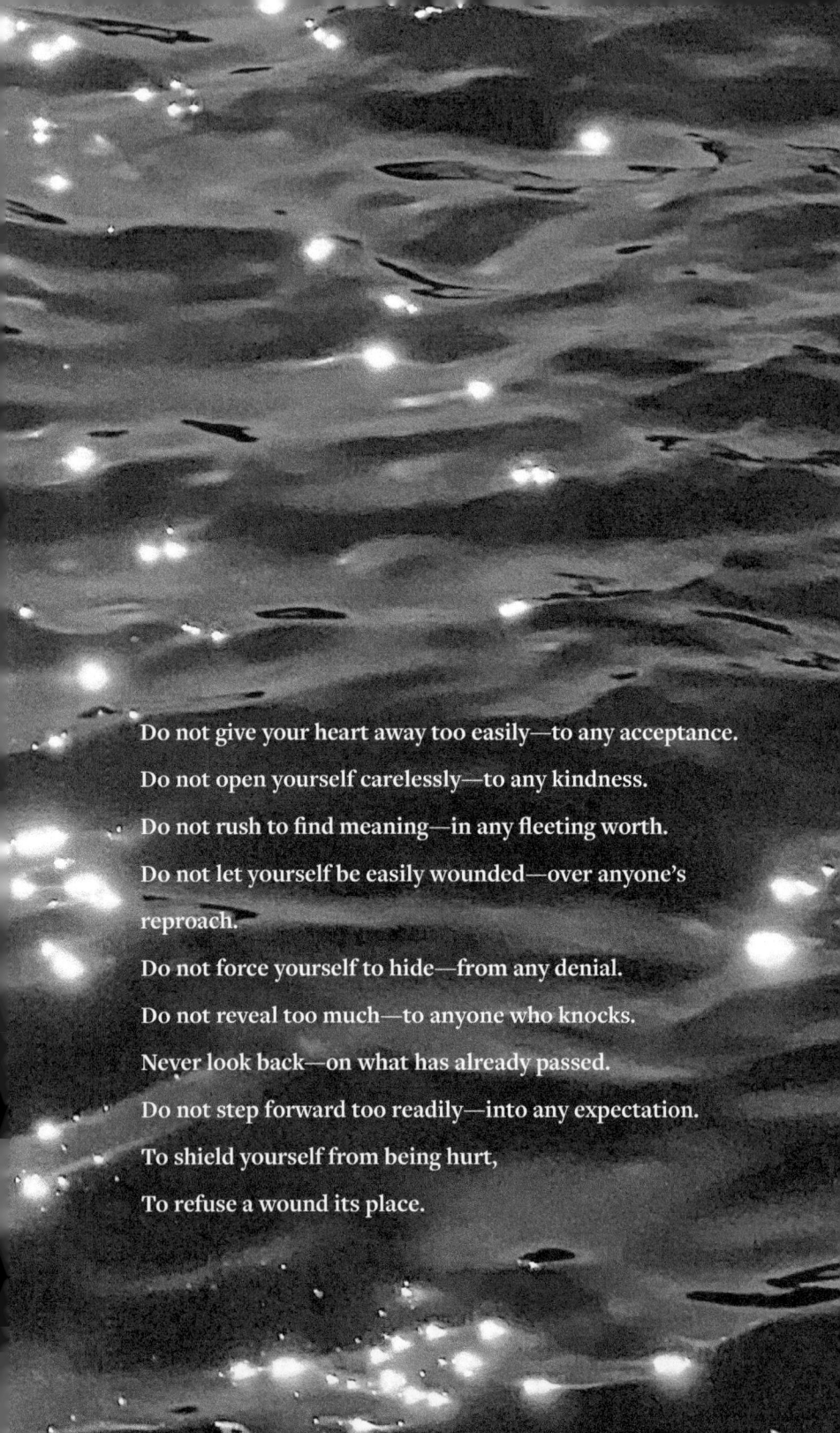

Do not give your heart away too easily—to any acceptance.

Do not open yourself carelessly—to any kindness.

Do not rush to find meaning—in any fleeting worth.

Do not let yourself be easily wounded—over anyone's reproach.

Do not force yourself to hide—from any denial.

Do not reveal too much—to anyone who knocks.

Never look back—on what has already passed.

Do not step forward too readily—into any expectation.

To shield yourself from being hurt,

To refuse a wound its place.

You May Run, You May Look Away

Even the strongest of hearts can carry deep pain when hurt by someone they've met. There are times when love feels like a language we've forgotten, when our hearts flinch at its touch. In these moments, rather than forcing ourselves to believe again, we can allow our hearts the space to retreat, to shield themselves, to breathe—if only for a while. You don't have to force yourself to trust or love if you're not ready.

And yet, someone always appears. Someone who makes you turn back, even as you keep walking away. Someone who, though seemingly severed from you, leaves behind the faintest thread—a thread that, one day, will quietly reconnect you.

I call them the one who makes you believe in love again. The one who revives even the smallest trace of warmth within you. Like a ginkgo tree standing firm through every season, they remain in the same place, unmoved by your refusals. With a tender smile tinged with longing, they will ask, "What beauty did you find in your brief escape?"

Yes, they exist—someone warm enough to understand the ways you are broken, someone patient enough to tend to those fragile pieces. So, listen to your heart's whispers of weariness, for sometimes, admitting you are broken is the first step toward healing. And never be afraid of being the villain in someone else's story.

My dear, there's something you must always remember. There may be those who help you along the way, but no one can live your life for you. So you must take care of yourself. Mind your health, tend to your heart. You must learn to care for yourself.

And above all—never live solely for others. No, never.

Live for yourself first and help others when the time is right.

Even I, your mother, after more than 60 years of life have lived over 60 years, still must swim through loneliness, life, health, and happiness—all on my own.

Do you understand?

Life is precious precisely because we alone are responsible for it.

- Words from my mother as she dropped me off at the lecture hall -

V

On Sadness and Shadows

Misfortune, Not Invited

I had a friend who lived in constant worry over their aging dog. Every day, they took the dog to the vet, saying they were preparing themselves for the inevitable. Then one day, they called me in tears. Their beloved companion had suddenly crossed the rainbow bridge. They had gone to sleep as usual, only to wake and find their companion lying there, no longer breathing.

"Suddenly," my friend kept saying.

Hearing that word over and over—"suddenly"—made me wonder: maybe all sorrows truly come this way, without warning. Even if we know, even if we try to prepare, it still strikes us out of nowhere. Perhaps we need to think of it as "sudden" so that we don't collapse under the weight of helplessness—so we don't hate ourselves for knowing yet doing nothing to stop it, so we don't feel foolish. Because there are still far too many things in this world beyond our control. And maybe we call those things, "miss fortune."

All misfortunes arrive unprepared, without invitation. It's not our carelessness or our stupidity—it's just the way our hearts choose to cope. Before we can say, "I did everything I could," the words spill out first: "It happened so suddenly." In a flash, before we know it, everything changes.

If I Could Go Back, Just Once

The times most precious aren't when we could say "I love you," but when we could still say "I'm sorry." Those fleeting moments when we still had the chance to ask for forgiveness, to plead, "I'll do better—don't leave me."

Even if someone was on the verge of walking away, at least there was a moment to atone for all the wrongs we'd done.

My mother once said that, in all her life, whenever something truly precious slipped away, all she could do was sink to the floor and weep. Not because she couldn't say "I love you," but because she could no longer say "I'm sorry" for the mistakes she'd made—no one was left to hear it. That was why she cried; there was nothing else she could do.

Before her mother's funeral portrait, at the grave of her cat that crossed the rainbow bridge, and for the first love who left because they had grown tired of her—any time she let pride get in the way of an apology, the moment she was finally ready to say "I'm sorry," there was no one left to hear it. So all she could do was kneel and let her tears fall, heavy with everything she had left unsaid.

It Was 6:40 and
I Wanted to Live Like a Streetlight

There are days when I feel I might be crushed under life's overpowering weight. Whenever that happens, I say I want to die. It's not a private whisper—I say it aloud to someone else. When I do, they look startled, and I laugh it off with a joke: "Just for one year. I just want to die for a year and then come back."

When my breathing grows labored and I long to vanish somewhere—but can't, because of relationships and work—I suddenly find myself envying a streetlight that has gone dark.

It was sometime between summer and autumn when I woke up in a cold sweat from a bad dream. I'd apparently drifted off very late, yet when I woke it was just barely dawn, and the clock hands hadn't moved much from when I'd fallen asleep. The moment I pulled back the blackout curtains and opened the window, the streetlight outside flicked off, making the world even darker. Since bright morning was still some time away, the view outside without the streetlight felt gloomier than a deep night lit by lamps. The clock read 6:40. My half-asleep lover squinted and asked if I was really up already, then slipped back into slumber. I stood there for a while, staring blankly at the dark sky, muttering that I wanted to die like a streetlight.

Wanting to die like a streetlight meant wanting to become that extinguished lamp out there. It didn't mean I had some urgent reason to commit suicide, nor did I want my life to end in a random accident. Rather, I wanted to set aside—just for a moment—the burden of having to prove my existence has value. Like a streetlight switching off at a set time and simply standing silent, I wondered: could something remain firmly in place without always fulfilling a purpose? I wanted to be like a streetlight that clicks off with the sunrise: still standing tall, yet unnoticed—unpointed at, unseen, and unfelt. Then, when night falls again, able to shine once more as if nothing had changed.

Because I'm someone who frets even when my name comes up in passing or when I'm asked simple questions, I yearned for a life where I could flick off my own switch for a while, caring nothing about how others might see me. Like traveling with my phone turned off, I wanted to wander free of notifications. Like a temporarily dead streetlight, I wanted to keep breathing while switched off—finding a quiet compromise with life.

I still often think about wanting to go dark like a streetlight. No—I think about wanting to live like a streetlight.

Because in this day and age, so many people struggle under the ever-shining light of youth that they just can't turn off.

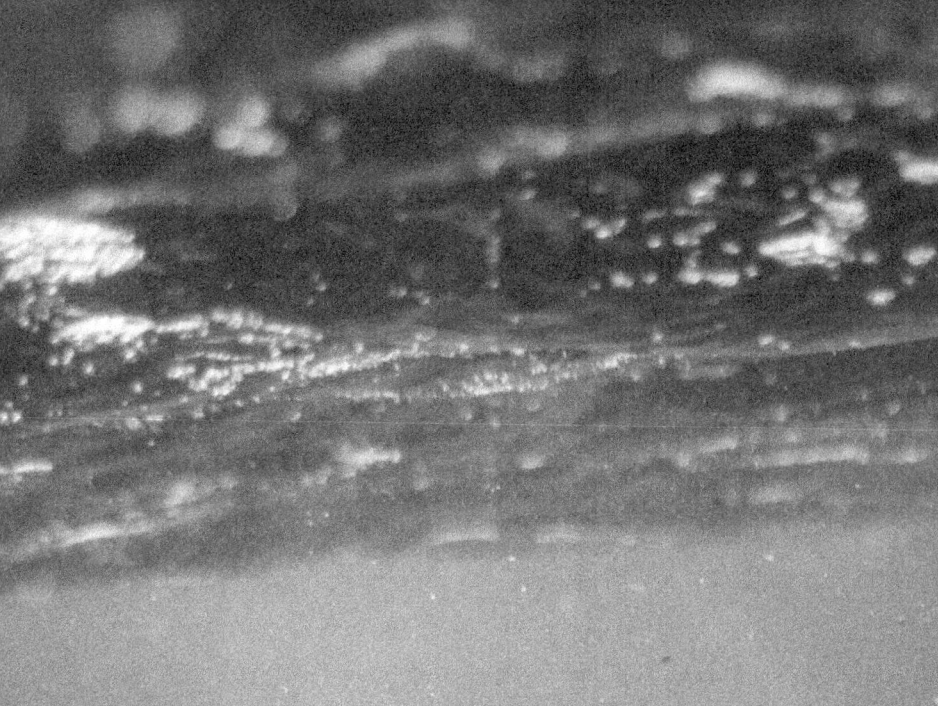

I know your sorrow.

But we must not drown—

Keep swimming, keep swimming

Until we break free of earth's pull.

My heart, all sharp corners and quiet edges,

Still Believes there must be boundaries

Even to an ocean of despair.

And on the days when we can barely stay afloat,

Even if we must swallow every drop of this sea,

Let us not sink beneath the waves.

System Failure:
Unplugging for a Moment

Somedays, I just want to declare myself officially broken. To malfunction so visibly that anyone can tell I'm out of order—a day when nobody questions what I do and simply closes their eyes in quiet acceptance. I figure everyone must go through this: when neither body nor mind cooperates, yet no one notices. And because no one notices, I start assuming I must be fine enough and keep on enduring.

It's not that I want to break down because life still feels manageable. It's that I'm already broken beyond repair, but nobody seems to see it, and I'm forcing myself to keep going anyway. That's why there are days I want to break down. To be so powerless I can't even consider getting back up. To stop functioning without any false hope or needless cheering, just to rest for a while. So that people will think, "Ah, they're broken," and leave me alone. So I can lie around at home, sleeping and lathering my heart with a medicine.

The Inevitable in Life

Depression comes when we feel the force of the inevitable—those moments when we realize that no effort can alter the unchangeable. When we watch someone walk away, their fading into the distance, no matter how many times we reach for them. When we give everything we have, pouring out every talent, yet still cannot grasp our calling. When we offer our utmost kindness only to face derision from those around us. When we fight desperately between what we long for and what is, only to watch them drift further apart, slipping beyond our reach. In these moments, the weight of the inevitable seeps into our hearts, spreading like water stains, slowly taking the shape of sorrow.

This is why I stand with those who carry the weight of depression or anxiety, quietly bearing their unseen burdens. Those who have poured their energy into countless efforts, both external and internal. Those who continue to pour themselves out even when they have nothing left.

Perhaps these heavy feelings—this sorrow—are not signs of being lost in darkness, but proof that you are still moving, still pushing forward with quiet determination.

I truly hope we become people whose efforts bear fruit, even when life doesn't always go as we wish. I hope you'll come to see that this sorrow, now settled like water stains in your heart, is slowly becoming the quiet strength that will hold you up.

So, this sorrow—it is proof that you are truly alive. And this anxiety—it is the pulse of a heart that refuses to stop moving.

Now I Understand: There was a time I believed relationships could be held together by heart alone, and a time I learned they often cannot. I once believed wholehearted effort alone could conquer anything, until I realized that even with such effort, some things remain out of reach. We all stumble upon that moment when an uncomfortable process reveals stark reality. At that moment, we realize just how worn we have become—as though the world itself had taken sandpaper to us.

Sleepless Night

In those moments when I finally found the courage to be honest with my feelings, I often discovered more losses than gains. Now, like a moth-eaten blanket layered with regrets, I can no longer be honest even when I should. How could anyone truly know me when I barely understand my own heart?

Sometimes, memories of those who have already left suddenly feel so vivid—I wonder, are they still doing well?

And so I float through the deep center of a sleepless night. Though quiet, it is far from peaceful. My mind staggers like one intoxicated by sleeping pills, yet my eyes refuse to close in this endlessly long dawn. Everything—every thought, every action—feels impulsive. My fingers hover uncertainly over my phone, threatening to do something I might regret. The afterimages of people I've let go and the ambiguous gestures of those who've departed remain so clear that I wish I could embrace them all tightly, if only in a dream.

What exactly am I longing for? What am I missing? Even as I wind back through my past like a clockwork toy, my heart makes no progress—like broken footsteps marking time in the same spot, just growing louder. The world seems so vast, and everyone else appears to be moving forward while I struggle like someone on a hamster wheel—exhausting myself just to maintain my position.

Hearts That Open Wide

There are people whose hearts, once opened, seem to forget how to close. They might seem so distant, even emotionless, as if their ability to give and receive affection has somehow faltered. They are the ones who shield their boundaries so fiercely that they appear cold-blooded, yet to those they allow close, they shine brighter than the gentlest sunlight.

For them, cutting ties with someone they've once cherished feels as painful as tearing away a piece of their own soul. So instead, they choose to freeze their hearts entirely. Even when wounded by those they love, they find it nearly impossible to harbor resentment.

They are the ones who find comfort in rewatching the same films, who recognize their favorite songs from the very opening notes. They give away their most beloved books as though offering a window into their world, yet feel awkward when receiving gifts in return.

Though they yearn for such deep tenderness, they have become cautious of their own vulnerable hearts, now hide behind doors with countless locks, burdened by the fear that they may never be able to shut themselves off again.

These are the ones who love too deeply, and because of this, they are both heartbreaking and deeply endearing. They carry the weight of somber shadows on the outside, yet their inner world glows with a warmth that outshines the sun.

The Courage to Be Kind in Darkness

I now understand that truly kind people aren't endlessly positive or warm-hearted; rather, they are those who, despite their many dislikes, possess a profound sensitivity. They are resilient, able to endure hardships and make sacrifices, yet they seldom speak harshly or stir tension.

Their kindness is born from deep empathy, from recognizing that others might carry the same irritations they themselves endure.

Rather than allowing their heavier emotions to distort their perception, they face them head-on, determined not to be shaped by them. Their kindness doesn't flow from an overflow of affection or righteousness, but from the conscious effort to rise above the rudeness and selfishness they've encountered.

In truth, they find little joy in people, situations, work, or love, yet they persist in choosing kindness, as if in defiance of the darkness within. They resemble fairy tale heroes, enduring relentless trials for those they love, or perhaps, they are those intimately familiar with the world's shadows, striving to never become the villain. They plant seeds of hope in those around them, reminding others that even the fiercest storms will eventually pass. They are like the violet twilight that emerges only after rain—gentle, balanced, and fleetingly beautiful.

They are those who, having seen the deepest darkness, still choose the courage to shine the brightest.

The Proof of a Heart

There is no choice more cruel to the heart than trying to prove it to someone it will never reach. This isn't to say that every attempt to express our feelings is meaningless in the end. But offering your most cherished feelings to someone out of reach—and quietly expecting them to respond—is perhaps the gentlest way to destroy yourself. And to carry hatred for someone out of reach—that, too, is mine to confess:

tenderness that might have remained, and a scent that might have lingered, left behind instead as a stained path of karma.

A heart can only be felt—it can neither be definitively proven, nor expect proof in return.

I learned this from someone who once held a deep place in my heart yet left behind only despair: nothing devastates us more than misplaced expectations and relationships that could never return what we hoped for.

"What made you so down? Love?"

"Love played its part…"

"I used to get really low because of work I am on, but now, it's love. And somehow, whatever I make the purpose of my life ends up making me miserable."

"That's a sad thought… The things we turn our hearts toward are the ones that break us."

"Yeah. Life's a storm cloud."

What I Regret Most

What I regret most is giving my whole heart to someone who would never truly see it—no, someone who saw it and still chose to look away. To someone I could never reach, I reached anyway, leaving behind a life that was already too full to carry, just to stretch toward them. To someone too caught up in their own struggle, I cried out that I was hurting too—that I was trying, that I was breaking, that I needed them to see me.

To someone who tapped at me with nothing but fleeting curiosity, I opened up again, and bled again. To words that meant nothing, I listened. To confusion I didn't cause, I apologized. To someone who was gentle with everyone but me, I still hoped they'd be gentle—just once—for me.

And after chasing for so long, even at the cost of losing myself, I became not someone treasured, but just someone easy. That someone who I once adored had already vanished, yet I had fallen too far to stop, so I tricked myself into believing even the worst parts were worth loving.

Only when those feelings loosened their grip like handcuffs finally undone—did I realize: spending too long chasing someone who never turns around doesn't just make you lost in love. It makes you lost to yourself. You lose the compass that once led you home, to yourself. When there were so many others who would have held my hand the moment I reached out—why was it you? I regret the emotions and time I poured out, but most of all, I regret the pain itself.

The pain, I should have taken for someone who would actually see my suffering and embrace it.

The Hunger of the Heart

Within everyone lies an unfillable void—a hunger of the heart, you might say. Or more simply, emptiness. Yet some cannot bear to let this emptiness be, rushing to fill it.—seeking, watching, receiving, moving. They become captivated by glimpses of happiness on the internet, define their worth by the relationships they display, or chase after possessions empty of meaning.

But I do not believe that a life lived without pause—too busy for emptiness to creep in—is a life well lived. Often, my life feels overcast, shrouded in something nameless. Each day leaves behind a hollow space, urging me to fill it with anything that might bring a fleeting sense of satisfaction.

I admire the quiet resilience of those who choose not to run, but to sit with their emptiness. To accept the hollow places within—that is a life lived well. To embrace what feels small or insufficient—that is a soul moving forward. A life that doesn't rush to be filled, but knows to acknowledge and tend its own lack. A life that doesn't exhaust itself in hollow information or decorative overload,

In truth, emptiness touches everyone at times. Just as movement stirs physical hunger, the heart, too, hungers after giving too much of itself. But when you are physically hunger gnaws at your body, would you feed it rusted nails? The nourishment we offer our hearts must be chosen as carefully as the food we place on our tongues. A heart that swallows everything in sight, unable to distinguish sustenance from poison, will only shatter in the end. But a heart that accepts its emptiness walks forward with a quieter, deeper grace.

And so, this hunger of the heart—perhaps it is nothing more than a hush of a gentle spring rain.

When My Shadow Stands in My Place

I want to live as someone true to their own heart. Someone who reaches out when they want to hold on, and lets go with a quiet smile when it is time to say goodbye. Someone unafraid to say, *"I'm struggling."* Someone who does not hesitate to draw a line with a hardened expression when they are upset. Someone who can say, *"That hurt me,"* and let their emotions spill instead of swallowing them whole. Someone who, when in pain, allows themselves to whimper, to complain, to simply be human.

Someone who, even when hurting, finds the strength to tap—softly, hesitantly—on the one who caused the pain, and whisper, *"Please, don't hurt me like this."* It was never honest that I wrestled with— it was fear. Because every time I've been honest with my heart, the world has looked away. Is the world moving the wrong way, or am I the one walking off course? Is there even such a thing as an answer? Even now, at this age, I still fear being myself—so I wear a shadow over my face, an exhausting disguise I've come to depend on. What stands ahead of me is a tired shade, The lies I created have stood in for me so long that the truth of what I feel is clouded, dimmed—and it's hard to tell, in this darkness, what's truly mine.

To Be Tenderly Attached to Every Moment

I don't believe lingering is always a mistake. The real mistake lies in denying yourself that moment of longing—brushing it aside in the name of caution. So, when the time comes, let yourself hold on little longer, so let yourself stay, even if the world calls it foolish. Before love, before loss—let be as attached as your heart follows. When we turned away from our own, anxiously calculating the next step—perhaps those were not acts of wisdom, but a crueler kind of goodbye, leaving scars as an attachment itself ever could.

Days When It Seems No One Cares About Me

There are days when it seems no one is thinking of me. Days when I've closed the doors to my own heart, or when I'm caught in memories of many people who left my side and never returned. Days when I forget the version of myself who once loved and was loved in return. Days when I imprison myself within the walls of sorrow and cannot find a way out. On such days, I think of someone I once cherished deeply but cannot easily reach—someone who was perhaps even closer to depression than my own melancholy.

Did you sleep well through the dawn, without waking? Have you eaten properly? What songs are you listening to? Did you dress warmly enough before going out? It's a bit chilly outside. By the way, aren't you curious about my day? I had rice noodles today. The moon was beautiful in the evening sky, so I took a photo. I even found the strength to move forward again after pausing for a while. Did I do well? A bit hard to read.

In life, there are people we carry countless questions for, but somehow never get to ask. People we ache to see again, but can't quite bring ourselves to check in on. People we want so badly to tell everything to, but who always seem just out of reach.

I want to tell you this: you, too, are surely that person to someone. I believe that with all my heart. And I hope you'll find a way to reach out from that sadness that feels like it might never end. Even on the days when it seems like no one wonders about you, remember—someone out there is thinking of you, this deeply, this desperately.

No Matter How I Crumble, Unless I Cease to Break Down

Somewhere in my early thirties, there was a version of me who sighed endlessly, insisting I wanted to live well. It was a phase everyone goes through—a transitional time filled with anxiety. A time when I couldn't hide the hollow feeling in my chest. During one winter holiday season, although nothing in particular was happening, I kept clearing my throat, wondering if I was living properly. Night after night, I fell asleep and woke up clutching worries like: What if I'm being left behind while nothing much happens? What if I'm wearing out, rusting away? One by one, the people I had wanted close by drifted off to their own lives. Some got married, some held funerals—in that seemingly endless weave of meetings and farewells, I alone felt suspended on my *Sleep Number* bed, my life as unchangingly customized as its perfect support—stable, yet somehow empty. But that very uneventfulness weighed on me. I wasn't drowning in work, nor deeply wounded by anyone, but I still felt inexplicably busy and bruised, turning away from things and letting them slip past me.

That year—despite all my uncertainty—there was a bright spot. For the first time in my life, I gained something I could truly call mine. Until then, I'd had nothing to claim as my own, so this felt like a significant new beginning, a chance to rebuild the foundation of my life. With most of my savings plus a large bank loan, I bought a small building in Mangwon-dong.

The former owner remarked on how impressive it was to see someone "so young" doing this, and I couldn't help wondering if I still counted as young as I crushed out my cigarette on the outer wall.

"I'll open a cafe here," I said. When the remodeling contractor arrived, he explained that the aging interior walls had to be torn down for the space to look right. Nervously, I asked, "Won't it collapse?" He assured me they would only remove as much as would still stand—and proposed we install new support beams where the walls came down. I patted the soon-to-disappear old wall a few times, then agreed.

No matter how I crumble, unless I cease to break down.
No matter how I crumble, unless I cease to break down.
No matter how I crumble, unless I cease to break down.

I wondered if my life—worn thin by so many feelings, too exhausted to hold on to anything—could also be "taken apart just enough without collapsing." And then, if I could brace it with new supports—start again, as if everything were new. Even now, sometimes my uneventful life leaves me uneasy, as though I'm standing still. But whenever I feel I might be slipping backward, I try to take apart just a bit of my day, heavy with stale emotion, and greet what's left with a sense of newness.

Because my anxiety doesn't stem from a specific event, nor am I truly slipping behind, I don't make huge efforts to fix myself. I simply mutter to myself and trade each day for a fresh one:

"No matter how I crumble, unless I cease to break down."

Because I, Too,
Am Living as Myself
For the First Time

Overwhelmed, too much. Every morning when I open my eyes, it's the start of a day I've never lived before—and yet, somehow, negativity lingers between one day and the next, as if I've already failed this one too. I feel like I'm dragging along even those who despise me, matching their weight to the ticking of each relentless hour.

The words I've spoken have wounded others without meaning to, and for that, I've paid—facing criticism both in front of me and behind my back.

Even as kindness and comfort are offered, I wear the face of someone who's fine, while inside, my heart is quietly crying.

It's like climbing a steep hill with a broken joint, switching out batteries batteries every time the body gives out—just to delay the collapse a little longer. I've never held the world in my hands, and the world's never truly turned its back on me either. And still, I find myself veering between fleeting highs and lonely lows, happiness and depression, riding out the temperature swings of each day.

In the turbulence of emotional takeoffs and landings, I should ready myself once more for tomorrow's flight. I've started countless days, again and again, thousands upon thousands of times, which only means I've met just as many firsts.

And still, life feels unfamiliar. And fast. And cold.

I still don't know how one is supposed to live. I'm not sure how to carry on smoothly. It's not just you. And it's not just me. Maybe it's because we're all doing this for the first time—living as ourselves.

And even this day I've just begun—is a maiden journey I'm taking for the first time ever.

I came across an old man selling four-leaf clovers for $2 on the street.

"Can I really buy luck for 2 bucks?" I asked.

Without a word, he handed me a three-leaf clover instead. "This one's 3 bucks."

"Why is it more expensive?"

"That's the price of misfortune.
Luck comes freely, without strings.
But happiness?
To be happy, you've got to sell your misfortune to someone else."

My feet suddenly felt too heavy to move.
Had my happiness always been built upon someone else's loss?

Faith,
Hope,
and Love

I was born into a family where my father was a Christian and my mother honored her ancestors—my father's condition for marriage being that she follow his faith. As a result, our family motto was the quintessentially Christian phrase: Faith, Hope, Love. Having attended church since before I was even born, I never experienced ancestral rites or bowing at altars to pray for well-being.

If I had to choose one word to define my childhood, it would be fear. Ghosts, the dark, the stillness before dawn—those eerie things filled my early years. It started in my lower elementary school days, when I was a mischievous, carefree child.

During the Lunar New Year, we visited my maternal grandparents' home. Relatives gathered to perform ancestral rites, pouring liquor over the graves and burning incense, while our family simply offered a moment of silence in accordance with my father's faith. Perhaps annoyed by our restlessness, the adults sent us children to play. My cousins and I, full of energy, scrambled over the tombs, rolling around and laughing without a care. The adults would occasionally scold us from afar, warning that we'd be punished for such disrespect. But at that age, I never truly grasped why it was wrong; I just ignored their words and kept running around among the graves, playing hide-and-seek until dusk.

That night, I returned to my grandparents' house, still catching faint whiffs of incense in the air. Exhausted by the day's adventures, the scolding, and lulled by the warmth of the heated floor, I dozed off almost immediately. In the depth of that sleep, something strange happened.

A sudden jolt—like electricity—rippled between my right ear and neck. My eyes snapped open, but my body refused to move. I had never experienced anything like it. I was paralyzed, trapped between sleep and wakefulness.

We were deep in the countryside, with no streetlights to soften the murky darkness. That night felt especially bleak, and in the midst of my terror, I saw a ghost. It appeared, cursing me, pressing me down. I panicked, trying desperately to move even a single finger, whimpering to break free from this nightmare. Suddenly, my body jerked awake. I bolted upright and ran to my father, sobbing uncontrollably.

"Dad, I was asleep but couldn't move! A ghost showed up and held me down, saying it couldn't stand the sight of me... telling me I had to be punished."

My father, barely awake, spoke softly.

"My dear, when that happens, just call out to God. Say, 'God,' and it will disappear."

My father meant to comfort me, but his words only fueled my terror. If calling on God was the only answer, then the ghost I had seen wasn't just an illusion. My father was effectively telling me, Yes, ghosts really do exist in this world. The scolding from running across the graves earlier in the day, the warnings from the adults, the guilt of being told I'd be punished—all of it came flooding back That night, even in my father's arms, I lay wide awake, trembling until morning. Only when daylight broke and the world looked normal again did I finally fall asleep.

For several years after that day, I struggled to overcome my fear. Sleeping alone was a nightmare every day, and when I felt someone touching my feet, I ran to my parents' arms. I relied on medication at times, and fell asleep with my bed covered in soft, comforting stuffed animals.

One day, what finally shattered my fear wasn't anything new—but the very thing that had once plunged me into terror: sleep paralysis. One night, I fell asleep clutching the lion plushie I always kept by my pillow. And in the midst of that familiar, paralyzing state, it appeared—that same lion plushie. It was then I realized: this presence I had feared for so long wasn't a ghost at all. It had come from inside me.

From that moment on, as if by magic, I was freed from every trace of that lingering fear. Completely. All at once. Watching this long-held anxiety dissolve so suddenly, I couldn't help but ask myself: what was I so afraid of? A strange sense of futility—not despair, but release—settled in, along with the firm conviction that there are no ghosts in this world. And my heart felt astonishingly light.

Whenever life brings with it new waves of fear or pain, I return to that memory. The name of God that I used to whisper inwardly with faith, hope, and love while wishing for ghosts to retreat, my father's words, and that lion plush that freed me from fear.

Father, does God truly exist? Is there really such a thing as the divine? If so, does your faith, hope, and love all come from Him? What do you do when faith and hope themselves become terrifying? What if they spark the very fear they're supposed to quell?

You wanted to show me your faith and hope, but they gave me an almost feverish mental anguish. Looking back, it wasn't the so-called ghost or even the sleep paralysis that tormented me for years—it was your single remark. If only you had said, *Don't worry, it's just a weird dream everyone experiences sometimes,*

I might have brushed it off. Do you agree that, at times, not repeating a grandly positive message can be more reassuring?

During those endless nights when sleep eluded me, I must have whispered God's name dozens of times, but each attempt just brought another wave of panic. A simple lion plushy did for me what constant prayer could not. When life is frightening, what do we seek? Why do faith, hope, and love sometimes feel more like a terrifying affliction than a consolation? Living by faith in something unseen can make nonexistent threats seem all too real.

So tonight, I lie awake again, haunted by what I can't be sure is there—believing in things that may not exist, yet fearing them all the same.

I still sometimes recall those years, murmuring God's name with motionless hands pressed tight in prayer. Were faith and hope fueling my anxiety instead of dispelling it? I wonder if the things that once made me happiest might be the very things that hurt me the most.

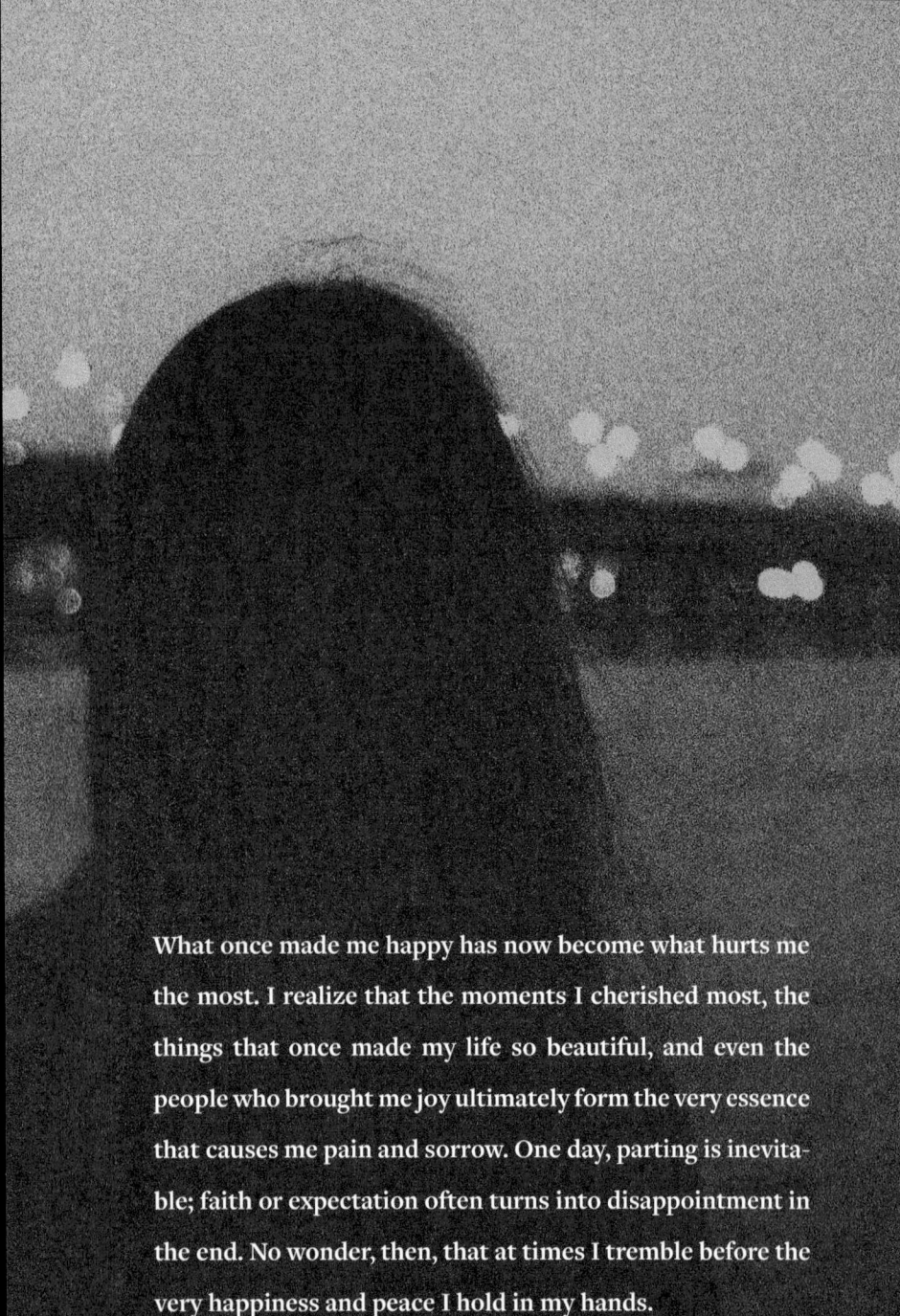

What once made me happy has now become what hurts me the most. I realize that the moments I cherished most, the things that once made my life so beautiful, and even the people who brought me joy ultimately form the very essence that causes me pain and sorrow. One day, parting is inevitable; faith or expectation often turns into disappointment in the end. No wonder, then, that at times I tremble before the very happiness and peace I hold in my hands.

Neither Sutured nor Flowing

I do not believe in those comforting phrases that say wounds heal with patience, or that hardships pass if only we endure.

The world does not work so kindly. It cuts deep and does not apologize.

The words and moments that once wounded me will continue to ache, and the pain will not simply fade away.

But there is one truth I hold:
with every bitter hour I endure, I become more grounded, more resolute.

The wound may not vanish, but it shrinks in power as my heart grows wide enough to contain it.

I may not escape it,
but step by steady step, I will walk through it,
not because time heals, but because I kept going, I believe.

It wasn't time that solved anything.
It wasn't luck that brought the end of sorrow.
It was me, standing firm, bearing it, surviving it.

I see your struggles without you speaking to them all, so I say to you:

keep believing, keep moving forward. Quietly and steadily.

To You Who
Are Someone's Light
And Someone's Sea

To you who wonder if anyone would recognize or mourn you if you died after such a seemingly meaningless life. To you who doubt whether anyone could ever love someone as insignificant as you. To you who blame yourself for not doing anything right and feel impatience creeping in. To you who feel so weak that even lifting the smallest thing becomes impossible, and that alone frustrates you. To you who see the world overflowing with reasons to look away. To you who, afraid of being ignored, end up doing things you yourself dislike—just to avoid being overlooked. To you who bow your head, uncertain if there's any point in continuing on like this.

As a well-known saying goes: the day you are living now is the tomorrow that someone who died yesterday so desperately wished to see. Stand firm against negativity, and refuse to cower before life's waves. Because you are someone's reason for hope and someone else's object of concern. Because you are your parents' vast ocean, your friends' exciting journey, and your lover's guiding light.

In moments when you refuse to give up, rising steadily even in your hardest times—when you lie face-down at rock bottom, yet still fight for air—when you keep swimming through a long tunnel instead of surrendering to despair: remember that the days you feel as chilling as a bitter cold or as faint as a slight fever, the days that seem nothing more than scattered crumbs, are the very days that help someone out there see you as lovable.

Never forget that someone in this world considers you worthy of pride. And on days when you believe there is no escaping your fears or your helplessness, remind yourself: right here, someone who has never even met you is cheering you on with all their heart. Because you are someone's light and someone's ocean. Because you are someone's future, and even a treasured past they long to recall. Because no one else can live your life for you, I hope you will live it wholly for yourself.

And to all who read these words—I hope you become someone you can be proud of.

"Wanna make a bet? Let's see who ends up happier."

"And For how long?"

"Until the day you win."

VI

We Shall Well Be

You Are Certainly Doing Well

You are doing well. You are living well. Though you haven't told yourself so, you truly are. The reason you can't tell yourself this is because your standard for 'doing well' has become perfection. Take a simple example: when we enjoy a meal, we say "I ate well," but this doesn't mean it was the most perfect meal ever. Sometimes, even with simple instant noodles, hunger makes them truly satisfying—more satisfying, even, than an expensive hotel breakfast. You see, 'doing well' is closer to satisfaction than perfection. So truly, in whatever situation or feeling we face, we are doing well. We manage our circumstances with quiet satisfaction, living contentedly within our lives. For instance, while there may be countless better-crafted sentences in the world than these simple words, because you are here, being moved by and reading them thoughtfully, even the writer is doing well in their own way.

I can say with certainty: you are, without doubt, doing well.

The Edge of A Coin

People often make decisions by flipping a coin, believing the odds of heads or tails are equal. But there is, in fact, a third possibility—the edge. A coin has three sides: heads, tails, and its edge. Yet because the probability of it landing on its edge is nearly zero, we never speak of it.

Life, too, holds such possibilities—ones that exist yet seem. Some worries are like a coin landing on its edge: technically possible, but so rare they are hardly worth considering. Still, since the probability isn't zero, we find ourselves unable to dismiss them entirely.

I call them "excessive worries."

If we step back, we'll see that life, much like a tossed coin, often spins beyond our control—yet we burden ourselves with fears as unlikely as a coin landing on its edge.

If we waste precious time fretting over near-impossible outcomes, while ignoring the far more likely ones—what could be more futile?

So, when extreme worry takes hold, just think of a coin landing on its edge. And just as we instinctively remember only heads or tails—forgetting the edge—let us also cast aside these needless fears.

Yes, we can force certain possibilities into existence, but unless we take deliberate action, they will never come to be.

Some things are simply too far-fetched to happen by chance. Excessive worries come to pass. May you never spend your days fixated on the edge, forgetting the far more probable heads and tails. Miracles do not happen as often as we might imagine. And as always, your path will be shaped not by the edge—but by heads or tails.

I cherish myself.

Rather than "stay strong,"

but to have the space along the way.

Rather than wishing for a life without hardship,

but a life where the struggles are worthwhile.

The Worry Worm

I know that concerns and worries sometimes serve to support life, but I also remain keenly aware that they are the very worms that erode at it. Worries grow by feeding on the peace within my mind. And when that inner peace runs dry, they begin to erode even the peace of my future.

That is why things that will never happen start to feel imminent, making us restless and uneasy. Everything is about balance, and there's nothing more important than balance when it comes to worry and anxiety.

Think, reflect, and even allow yourself to feel anxious. But if your thoughts do not lead to immediate action, let them go. That kind of worry is nothing more than an excess that serves no purpose.

You are stronger than you think, yet the worry worm within you keeps devouring your warmth, leaving only fragility and emptiness. If you lack the courage to act and change the situation right now, then—at the very least—pause your worries, if only for a moment.

Remember When Life Feels Overwhelming

Everyone Has Regrets

Remember that no matter what choices you make, life will always come with regrets and lingering what-ifs. You're not the only one who second-guesses decisions or feels a sense of loss—it's simply human nature to doubt. The closest thing to a right answer is to keep doing your best within the circumstances you're given. Regret doesn't mean failure; it means you're moving forward.

Compare, But Never Shrink Back

When you're around someone is more capable or excels in some areas, let it be a source of learning, not self-doubt. There is something that only you can do well—just as others have things only they can do. Comparing yourself to others is inevitable, but letting it shrink you is a choice. Comparison itself isn't the problem; what matters is whether you let it fuel your growth or drag you down.

Switch Off Your Thoughts for a While

It's okay if you haven't found a solution. Sometimes, the only way to ease the relentless tension between life and you is to let go. Even if you step back without resolving something, the effort you put into seeking a solution has already strengthened you. And sometimes, simply saying, *"Forget it,"* and allowing yourself to rest is its own kind of strength.

Your Only True Ally Is Yourself

At the end of the day, thank yourself for making it through, even if you stumbled and made mistakes. When life feels overwhelming, don't be harsh on yourself—take care of yourself with kindness. Keep telling yourself: *"Getting through a hard day is no small feat—I did well today."* In a world where allies grow fewer with time, remember—there's no better support than the one you give yourself.

Emotions Are a Resource Too

As we grow older, we learn to turn a blind eye to things—not out of ignorance or fear, but because we understand that sometimes, letting go brings the most peace. Don't waste your emotions where they don't belong. Save your energy for what truly matters, for the things that build rather than drain you.

Life is full of things that are difficult to understand or accept, and sometimes, that's just the way it is.

You're really doing well.

Without confidence, even things that could have gone well won't work out. So eat well, stand tall, and keep moving forward, take a deep breath, square your shoulders. Because really, what does it matter? If nothing else, let's not go through life feeling small.

Nothing Does So Just to Do So

Once, I wrote the sentence "Nothing does so just to do so" and found myself grinning with joy for having captured my philosophy of life in a single line.

Nothing grows merely to be eaten. Nothing fights merely to lose. Nothing cooks merely to taste bland. Nothing runs merely to fall behind. Nothing creates merely to break, and connects merely to be severed. Even when the results don't always align, the fact that nothing exists for the sake of a negative, guides me to a quiet solace.

Why do we cling to our countless worries, tormenting ourselves, while turning from this restful truth? Why do we blame ourselves so? Why do we regret so? No worry exists for the sake of decline. No fear exists for the sake of failure. All these are but fuel for moving forward. Even when outcomes suggest otherwise, let us move forward believing that nothing does so just to do so. By knowing this truth deep in our hearts, our lives will flourish—not for flourishing's sake, but because that is the way of life. Trust that all our countless worries and fears are but steps in the process of rising and moving forward.

So that struggle—yes, it's unfolding well. Those worries and fears—yes, you're living well. Even crawling on the ground—yes, you're moving forward well

Your own Season

You have your own season. We all have our own seasons. Though this is a truth everyone knows without need for explanation, it's not easily accepted—because until that season arrives, life's apparent futility, where effort shows no visible rewards, torments us relentlessly.

At such times, what we can do is neither conjure magic to hasten our season nor forcefully create opportunities by relying on others. Even less should we abandon all our efforts so far, simply because we can't wait for our season. We just need to keep going steadily, repeating to ourselves that each of us truly does have our own time.

So, let me remind you: there is a season—each has their own. Even flowers that bloom and wither in a single spring wait an entire year in dormancy before their brief display.

Even the tiniest insects remain cocooned, holding their breath until the day they can spread their new wings. Never forget that everything alive has its season—including the fact that your own season may not have arrived yet.

When to Entrust the Time

Life is an ongoing process of chipping away at the rigid beliefs we once clung to. One day, what we deemed correct might prove wrong; another day, what we dismissed as a mistake could turn out to be right. Thus, life is about realizing that even the answers we believed in might not be real answers at all, and that genuine solutions can sometimes emerge from where we saw no answers at all.

Yet this process does not always flow according to our wishes. Growth and understanding rarely happen overnight. That is why, at times, we must entrust certain matters to the passage of time. After enough days or even years, we might end up discarding ideas we once found irrefutable, or accepting what we had long denied. Some things remain utterly beyond our grasp no matter how hard we strive in the present—only time can gradually unravel them. I'm not one to say, "Just go with the flow," but there are moments when even our fiercest efforts lead nowhere, and the only remaining path is to let time take its course.

Knowing when to leave certain things to time allows us to invest our energy in pursuits that truly matter. It helps us avoid wasting effort and keeps our emotions intact.

"The power of time is stronger than we imagine."

Or, to put it more precisely:

"Often, the power of the time we have endured surpasses even the mightiest effort we can muster in the moment."

A tree is not bad because it bears no fruit.
A tree is not good simply because its fruit is plentiful.
A true tree is one that may sway in any storm
yet never breaks.

Your efforts are the roots that support you deeply.
You need only remain unbroken.

Do not call yourself a dead tree just because you've borne no fruit. And do not boast simply because your harvest is abundant.

Remember this as you journey through life:
All effort becomes not the fruit of success,
But the unbreakable strength to endure.

Life's Signposts

Everyone has a first—maybe the first time they tasted spicy tteokbokki, or the first Christmas present they ever received. We might not know for sure whether these were truly our earliest experiences, but in our memories, they remain so. In that sense, my "first trip" was the one I took with my father to the nearby countryside.

He'd spread out a map, announce that we were going on a trip, then load me into his bright red
Pride and head out. "I'm sure this is the right way," he'd say confidently. And, without wandering too far off course, we'd actually arrive at our destination. "See? Dad can find anything!" he'd declare, sliding a proud hand across his nose. I was too young for elementary school, just a tiny kid gawking at a dizzying map that my father could read effortlessly. To me, he was like Superman—I looked up at him in awe and asked how a map worked.

He pointed here and there, explaining that to go south, you simply move downward on the map; to go west, you track left.

If something was located east, you just headed right. I stared at him with wide, skeptical eyes—could it really be that easy? Then he rested his hands on my small shoulders and said, "If you know where you want to go, the rest doesn't matter so much."

"It's easy, son. If you know where you're headed, just keep going—Sooner or later, you'll find a signpost!"

Thinking back to that first trip with my father, I remember about when I took my first steps into society, away from his side. My uncertain youth—always rushing as if being chased, never quite sure whether this path was right, whether to keep running or turn back, floundering in indecision. As an adult, to arrive at my destination with the same certainty my father once had. I wanted to move forward with grace, even on a road filled with uncertainty—one with vague directions, restless anxiety, tempting shortcuts, and winding, unpaved paths. I wanted to be kind of adult who, even after taking a few detours and wavering a bit, could eventually arrive, smooth my nose bridge, and proudly say, "Look at this."

If I could tell my younger self just one thing, it would be the same simple advice my father once gave me—just keep moving toward your destination. On days when I'm plagued by doubts in thoughts like "Am I going the right way? Am I falling behind?"—I remind myself of his words. If you keep going in the direction of your destination signposts will appear.

To you who stand before a beginning, to you who might still be circling the starting point—this is the small encouragement I wish to offer. Don't worry too much. Life's signposts will reveal themselves in time. Just keep moving forward.

Do not let your desires for what you want rest easy.

Like a wild giraffe, you must sleep standing.

And live while adapting to countless poverty.

Learn to drink muddy waters sweetly

until you become immune.

Do not turn your back on long-held dreams.

Someday you'll count all the stars in the sky—

let them mock as you look up.

You will succeed in love.

Like your father's worn Bible, do not discard it,

And remain devoted to protecting and being protected.

Someday you will serve your family.

Though parents and siblings don't beg,

approach first and watch over them.

Walk yearning for wisdom.

Look upon and experience the truth

unchanging like a mother's love.

Live with upright conviction,

like something that will grow tall even if bent for a moment.

Establish your own laws but do not settle within them.

Like a giraffe's neck—proud and straight—

As if it had never been otherwise.

Living Well Means

All around me, life barely stirs—like a punch I'm desperate to throw at someone I dislike in a dream, yet can't quite land. Though I'm not actually drunk, I often stumble over the words I wish I could say. And although my gaze is fixed straight ahead, each day I wobble as if walking on an unsteady ankle. It is to be said that the life is mine to steer, yet it veers left when I turn right, and right when I turn left.

Still, I believe. Like an embrace offered in a dream to someone I could never truly reach, there must exist a life that can ultimately cradle even what I've failed to achieve. It's like the quiet lightness of heart brought on by a refreshing breeze when I'm pleasantly tipsy on my way home, or the unplanned delight of stumbling onto a lovely flower garden. There are no sure signposts in the path I take; maybe that's why we all keep going, somehow managing our anxiety in the face of not knowing where we're heading.

Indeed, living well means being able to find restful sleep—whether we dream of things damp with unease or softly comforting. It means moving forward with mindful steps, grateful that our stumbles aren't so dire as to collapse our foundations. It is washing away old misfortunes with a stroke of unexpected luck. And it's about traveling our own true road, holding on to the hope that, precisely because life doesn't always go as planned, it might turn out even better than we dared imagine.

Truly, that is what living well means.

Though I Can't Remember Your Voices

When I was very small and insignificant yet precious,
The fruit of two people's care and nurturing,
A fragile pinky finger and a thumb to be proud of—
Back when I had just learned to roll over, crawling on all fours,
Then toddling along only to fall and let out a cry,
There were voices I cannot remember yet cannot forget.
"Can you stand up again, little one?"
Voices that would come whenever I fell and rose again.
"You're doing so well. That's right. That's right."
Though I don't remember your voices from then,
Look how well I am moving forward now.
I've grown so well that I can carry you both on my back
And still walk steadily on my two feet.
All thanks to those voices from back then.
We all started with unsteady first steps to arrive
where we are today.
Just as those small voices lifted me
then to become who I am now,

The quiet encouragement I give myself today
Will someday lift me up and pull me toward who I am meant to be. Not forgetting those voices from then, you now say to yourself:
I can stand up again. I am doing well. Let's keep moving forward just like this.

The Green Light Towards Your Life

When the traffic light turns red, we stop.

When it turns green, we move forward.

If the light is green yet those around us remain still, hesitating alongside them would be foolish. No one pauses at the edge of a crosswalk, doubting whether they should cross when they already know the signal allows them to go. We trust the meaning of a green light—we step forward without question because we are certain of what it signifies.

That certainty: If we hesitate despite the green light before us, perhaps it is not the path that is unclear but our own conviction that falters. I wonder—have I been living my life without that certainty? Have I been stopping simply because others stop, drifting merely because the world drifts? Have I, out of doubt, failed to act upon what I have always known to be true?

Trust the green light ahead of you: More than that, trust yourself, trust that what you see is green, that your instincts are not mistaken. Do not measure your steps by those around you; let your heart be the compass that guides you.

To move forward in life requires only one thing: not the world's approval, not external validation, but the quiet, unwavering certainty within your own heart.
And even now, look—it shines before you.

The green light, waiting for you to take that step.

Though to me the waves are what crash,

To the waves, I am the obstacle in their path.

Come to think of it, to trials I am what must be overcome,

What must be broken down, and what must be met as well.

In the midst of fierce sea winds and vast waves.

"I am the trial for the trials."

I will not forget this.

Setting Sail

There are times when unforeseen misfortunes try to drag me into the depths. Times when sorrow, fierce and unexpected, pushes me toward collapse, and I struggle with all my might to resist. Life's waves rise higher than I ever imagined, their depths surpassing the limits of my endurance—moments when I flounder, swallowing the briny weight of my own unshed tears.

In such times, I recall the story of a captain navigating the vast, open sea, a story no one ever told me, yet one I have always known. When the winds howl with the force to tear my heart asunder, when those very winds turn to waves that crash upon my life, that is when I must raise the anchor and unfurl the sails, setting my course toward the boundless horizon.

Raise the anchor!
Unfurl the sails!
We are setting sail!

May we never remain motionless in the face of hardship. May we not cower before the tempests of misfortune, allowing ourselves to be shattered by fear. Even if our vessel is but a humble sailboat, may we stand resolute, facing the storm, forging ahead.

Like a veteran captain who knows what must be done even with a disoriented heart, I resolve to transform crisis into opportunity.

No matter where it leads, let us set sail. With the belief that raising anchor serves not to regress, but to advance. With faith that the sails exist not to be torn, but to endure. And with trust that this endurance will guide me to somewhere clearer than the world of today. Hoping all these beliefs become tomorrow's compass, beyond the dizzying today.

Straighten your hunched back and lift your head high!
Spread your arms wide and open your heart!
We are setting sail!

www.ingramcontent.com/pod-product-compliance
Lightning Source LLC
LaVergne TN
LVHW011946060526
838201LV00061B/4229